STRESSLESS LIVING

STRESSLESS LIVING

*Release the Pressures of Life and Start
Enjoying Every Day*

by
Lindsay Roberts

Harrison House
Tulsa, Oklahoma

06 05 04 03   10 9 8 7 6 5 4 3 2 1

StressLess Living: Release the Pressures
of Life and Start Enjoying Every Day
ISBN 1-57794-584-0
Copyright © 2003 by Lindsay Roberts
Oral Roberts Ministries
Tulsa, OK 74171-0001

Published by Harrison House, Inc.
P.O. Box 35035
Tulsa, Oklahoma 74153

Contents

CHAPTER 1

The Ride of Your Life

Chloe was doing her best to be brave. "I can do it, Mom. I can do it!" she insisted.

Our daughter was only eleven, yet she was facing a tense situation.

As a mother, I knew she wasn't ready for this—and I wanted to stop her. At the same time the Spirit of God was saying, "Don't you dare! It will help her grow up." That morning, as we were driving to the big event, Chloe decided to sit in the third seat of our family car—way in the back. On the second seat were her sisters, Jordan and Olivia.

The Spirit of God was saying, "Don't you dare! It will help her grow up."

We had been driving only a few minutes when suddenly Chloe screamed, "Stop the car! Stop the car! I'm going to throw up!"

There were no windows in the back of our car, so she jumped forward to the middle seat. Seconds later, Olivia realized what was about to happen. Anxious to get out of the way, she quickly jumped on Jordan's lap and sat on her sister's breakfast. Olivia had a cheese sandwich smashed on her backside. And the rest of it was smeared on Jordan's front side.

Immediately, I pressed the button to roll down the window and shouted, "Chloe, just lean over and throw up outside!"

So what does Chloe do in her distress? She turns to throw up directly in Jordan's and Olivia's laps.

Instinctively, thank God, Olivia grabbed her, stuffed her head out the window, and Chloe continued heaving out the car window for the next several blocks.

Running Like Jackrabbits

When we arrived at our destination, I tried to be dignified, calmly asking, "Can you please tell me where the nearest restroom is located?"

By my side was Chloe, screaming, "Bathroom! Bathroom!" Someone pointed in the right direction, and we ran like jackrabbits.

"Mom, get me a trash can," Chloe begged, as she found a place to sit. Of course, the container was attached to the wall, so I ripped the plastic garbage bag out of the bin and rushed it over to my nauseated daughter.

When her vomiting finally subsided, I took some water from the sink and rubbed it over my little girl's face. Putting both arms around her, I gave up and said, "Let's just go home now."

To my shock, and really in rebuke, Chloe pulled away from me, squared her shoulders back, and stood up. She wiped her face and, with great determination, said, "I'm ready. Let's go do this!"

If you're breathing, stress will find you.

A Guarantee

Chloe taught me an important lesson that day. As you will discover in this book, the issue is not avoiding stress— we all experience tension that can tie our stomachs in knots. It is how we react under pressure that builds our character, strengthens our moral fiber, and develops our inner strength.

I truly believe that if you're breathing, stress will find you. It's almost a guarantee. However, there comes a time in life when you must decide to step to the next level.

Will it be easy? Heavens no.

Will you react? Or will you respond?

That's up to you.

- *When you react, stress controls you.*

- *When you respond with the Word of God, you take control over stress.*

It really is up to you. God has already done His part. The question now is, Are you ready to do yours?

A Horse Named Wisdom

Chloe's response to stress should not have surprised me because this certainly was *not* the first time she'd experienced the opportunity to put stresses to the test. I can still remember seeing my little daughter at the age of seven entering her very first horse riding competition. All of our girls have taken riding lessons, and Chloe longed for the chance to enter her first competition.

The horse she was riding was an Arabian that was about thirty years old and really ready for retirement. This was a tired, worn-out horse, and she was only going to walk and trot him around the arena.

But this wasn't just any horse—this horse was Wisdom. As a concerned mom with a little girl onboard a big horse, I felt a great deal of confidence that my baby would be gently trotting around the arena on *Wisdom*. I mean, he couldn't be named Wisdom for no reason, right? Wrong.

A Strong-Willed Horse

As proud parents, we were in the stands watching little Chloe enter the arena on her mount.

When Wisdom reached the center of the arena with the other horses, he suddenly realized he was an Arabian and wanted to prove it. It was as if Wisdom regained his youth— he began cantering like a crazy horse. Wisdom, nothing.

If you have ever ridden an Arabian, you know that they are extremely strong-willed and often difficult to handle. So there we were, unable to help our little girl, watching Wisdom as he took off like a rocket with Chloe bouncing to high heaven. He was as excited as popcorn kernels on a hot stove, colliding into the other horses and frightening everyone in sight.

"Whoa! Whoa!"

Richard and I jumped to our feet, and I was praying, "O Jesus, please help my baby not to fall." We were terrified beyond words.

Chloe was screaming at the top of her lungs, "Whoa! Whoa! Stop! Stop!"

Wisdom completely ignored her. After showing off, he headed straight for one of the exits and ran out of the arena.

Richard and I quickly followed Chloe outside and could see she had burst into tears. Our daughter was tough, but this was too much. Someone yelled, "Why didn't you control your horse?"

There was no applause. There would be no ribbon. There was nothing but tears.

As she stood next to Wisdom, my heart was breaking. I thought, *My poor little girl. She's so humiliated.*

But, to our surprise, Chloe grabbed Wisdom by the bit, jerked his face to hers, looked him straight in the eyes, and said, "Why did you embarrass me like that in front of all these people? Don't you ever do that to me again."

We were speechless. Was that our little girl talking like that? Inside, I was saying, *You go, girl!* I realized that she was only a child, but the weapons of her warfare were mighty.

Peace doesn't mean you don't go through anything; it simply means how you end up after you've gone through something.

It was amazing to us how quickly she bounced back from a moment of extreme distress. Somewhere, somehow, she had learned some valuable lessons and had them hidden deep in her heart. In crisis, they were immediately available as she drew from down deep within herself and pulled out that inner strength placed there by God Himself. Out of it, she grew, we grew, and God was glorified.

A Basket Case?

Those who know me well may wonder, *How can Lindsay Roberts write a book about stress?*

I confess that I'm often a basket case. As my husband, Richard, likes to say, "If patience is a virtue, Lindsay is virtue-less."

The other side of the coin is that you can't talk about anything you haven't experienced. And, oh, have I experienced pressure, stress, and anxiety.

Then you begin to realize that peace doesn't mean you don't go through anything; it simply means how you end up after you've gone through something. I have said many times that truly sometimes God delivers you *from* the fire. However, there are many times He delivers you *through* the fire.

The bottom line is that God delivers. How that comes, and sometimes whether or not it comes at all, largely depends on how we react or respond in the midst of the trial. It isn't always possible to live without stress, but I believe it's possible to live *through* it triumphantly.

My Question

One day I asked the Lord, "Am I going to have to go through *everything?*"

He responded, "No, just the things you're going to share with others."

On these pages I want you to see:

- How to move from stressing to blessing.

- The miracle of joyful living.

- The secret of thinking from your heart and not your head.

- The power of diligence.

- How to find strength in the midst of a crisis.

- How to overcome fear and anxiety.

- Eight steps that can lead to victory.

I pray that this book will cause you to realize that the trials you walk through are a training ground—not to fulfill your desires but to lead you to the amazing place God wants you to be.

CHAPTER 2

The Joy of Knowing

Have you ever slipped on an icy street or flattened your-self because of a slick floor? Oh, how it hurts, physically and emotionally.

There's no thrill in scraping your knees or bruising your ego. Yet I've heard people quote the Scripture that reads, "My brethren, count it all joy when ye fall..." (James 1:2).

Hold it. That's not the message James was writing to believers. He wasn't saying, "Be happy when you stumble and mess up your life." Not at all. And if you aren't happy when you fail, keep reading and uncover one of the most priceless nuggets in God's Word.

James wrote, "My brethren, count it all joy when ye fall into divers temptations; knowing this, that the trying of your faith worketh patience" (James 1:2,3).

The two key words are *knowing this.*

- The joy is not in falling.

- The joy is in *knowing this.*

The word *patience* means "hopeful endurance, constancy, continuance, waiting, calm endurance of hardness, capacity, provocation of pain, tolerance, perseverance, forbearance, diligence, tenacity, doggedness, self-possessed waiting."

God is working things out for our good, and that's not just a master plan—it's the Master's plan.

Then the Scripture goes on to tell us to "Let patience have her perfect work, that ye may be perfect and entire, wanting nothing. If any of you lack wisdom, let him ask of God, that giveth to all men liberally, and upbraideth not; and it shall be given him" (James 1:4,5).

What an exciting plan to move from *stressing* to *blessing.* Instead of failing, the Word tells us we can be *complete, perfect, made whole,* and *wanting nothing.* How does it happen? Through the joy of *knowing.*

And what do you know? God has a master plan that "all things work together for good to them that love God, to them who are the called according to his purpose" (Rom. 8:28).

It does not say that all things *are* good. However, it says all things work *together* for good. For whom? For those who love the Lord and are called according to His purpose. God is working things out *for our good,* and that's *not* just *a* master plan—it's *the* Master's plan. It's God's blueprint for our lives.

A Blueprint That Works

In math we all learn that two plus two equals four. And every time we add those numbers the result is the same. However, if we change the *plus* to a *minus,* we destroy the formula, and the answer becomes quite different.

God has given us a plan and a purpose—plus a specific procedure to fulfill that plan. It's called the Word of God. As we pour ourselves into the Scripture, we soon begin to understand that God's blueprint will work again and again.

There are two reasons we can trust what our heavenly Father declares:

1. **The Word is truth.** "God is not a man, that he should lie" (Num. 23:19).

2. **The Word never changes.** God declared, "I am the Lord, I change not" (Mal. 3:6).

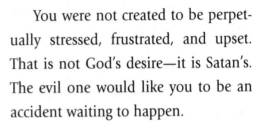

I really do know what it's like to live under intense stress. In fact, if the old saying is true that experience is the best teacher, I'm well taught.

You were not created to be perpetually stressed, frustrated, and upset. That is not God's desire—it is Satan's. The evil one would like you to be an accident waiting to happen.

But the Lord sees you living in victory. The Word declares, "The Lord shall make thee the head, and not the tail; and thou shalt be above only, and thou shalt not be beneath" (Deut. 28:13).

How is such a life possible? It comes not only by the Word of God, but by *applying* the knowledge of God's Word.

Remember that James 2:26 says "faith without works is dead." Once we get a word, an insight, or a revelation from God, then we must do something with it. And that something is to put it into action and apply it to our lives.

It's a lot like makeup. It's wonderful to have a drawer full of it but, oh, what a difference it can make when you actually apply it. God's Word is just the same.

A Shocking Report

After a seminar, I was stopped by a woman who told me, "I loved what you had to say, but you could never *really* understand the pressure I'm under."

Before praying with the woman I replied, "Believe me. I *totally* understand what it's like to live with stress."

Yes, I really do know what it's like to live under intense stress. In fact, if the old saying is true that experience is the best teacher, I'm well taught.

When Richard became President of Oral Roberts University in the early 1990s, the accountants gave him a report that was more than shocking. He was told, "The university is over $50 million in debt, and we are not sure there is any way out."

Day after day, night after night, I watched my husband nearly crushed under the heavy burden of debt, devastation, and a host of other problems hitting all at the same time.

He would come home daily declaring, "I've been a fireman all day long. All I do is put out fires." In fact, he said this so many times that when our youngest daughter was asked what her daddy did for a living she honestly replied, "He's a fireman!"

Enrollment at ORU was decreasing, the bankers and creditors were coming from both sides, squeezing like a vise, and Satan was telling him, "The world is sure going to laugh when these doors are bolted shut."

The vultures began to circle, and perhaps the most hurtful shock came to me when some Christian ministries were hovering, waiting to seize the property for pennies on the dollar.

Almost immediately, the pressure began to take its toll. Richard was weakening physically. He developed an ulcer that affected his eating, he wasn't sleeping at all, and I was crying myself to sleep. We had never experienced such heartache and anguish. The debt seemed like a life sentence. We were living a nightmare.

Like a Dead Man

In those desolate days, the girls and I would literally scatter when Richard came home from the office—waiting to see what mood he might be in.

My husband is not the kind of person who would rant and rave or pound the floor. He just fell silent or would quietly walk off talking to himself. Most nights he would come home exhausted—like a dead man walking. I would hurt so deeply because there was nothing I could do to help. I couldn't fix the problem and neither could he.

One afternoon, in an effort to lighten the situation, I told the girls that we were going to play a little game called, "Let's celebrate with Daddy." I said, "No matter how he is feeling when he gets home, we're going to make him feel great."

We knew that one of his favorite meals at home was oriental chicken stir-fry. It only takes a few minutes to cook but a long time to cut up and prepare the ingredients. So the girls and I went to work chopping the chicken, the vegetables, and all that fancy stuff I throw in. We set a beautiful table that anyone would have been proud of.

Suddenly–POW!
The gas exploded
and blew me
across the room.

I Became a Human Rocket

Richard phoned and said, "I'll be about ten minutes late, but I'm on my way."

Perfect, I thought. *We'll cook it now and have it on the table piping hot the minute his feet walk through the door.*

We have a gas grill in our kitchen, and I turned it on. But I couldn't immediately find the little portable flame lighter. When I finally located it, I flicked it on and touched the flame to the grill—not realizing I had left the gas on far too long. Suddenly—POW! The gas exploded and blew me across the room. I hit the wall with a thud.

The girls came rushing over to me, and when they realized I wasn't dead, they burst into laughter. Mom became a human rocket right before their eyes.

Thank God I was wearing a pair of thick, heavy-rimmed glasses that protect my eyes.

Olivia said, "I wonder what Daddy will think?"

"What do you mean?" I responded.

"Well, just look at yourself." she laughed.

When I looked in the mirror, I couldn't believe it. My eyebrows were singed off, and the front of my hair was singed off completely. I did not have a "bad hair" day. I had a "no hair" day. You could smell it burning.

Again, Olivia wondered, "What's Daddy going to say?"

"He probably won't even notice." I responded.

Let the Games Begin

So we made a game of it, and I said, "Let's play 'See if Daddy will notice that Mommy blew her hair off today.'"

The rules were simple. "You can't tell him, and you have to keep a straight face. If he doesn't notice by the time dinner is over, I'll take you out on a shopping spree."

The rules were set, and we couldn't wait to play. Unfortunately, in my heart I knew how Richard had been acting lately, and I truly believed I had already won. I was sure he wouldn't even notice.

Minutes later, in walks Richard, and he's in one of his silent moods. That means you don't say anything until he comes to the table, and then you give him ten extra minutes.

We sat down at the table, and the stir-fry vegetables were ready—hot and perfect. We had fluffy rice and all the extras. It was delicious.

"I blew my hair off with the gas grill. I have almost no eyebrows. I'm bald where I used to have bangs, and my hair smells like it's singed."

Richard had almost finished his dinner, yet he had not uttered a word. The girls, however, could hardly contain themselves. Finally they started giggling out loud, and I knew I had to say something.

"Richard," I began, "do you notice, anything different about me today?"

He looked me straight in the face and said, "No."

Now, mind you, the front part of my hair was singed and brittle and actually smelled like burning hair, and my eyebrows were singed as well.

One of my daughters fell on the floor laughing at this point. So I repeated, "You don't notice anything different about me?"

He looked at my very old, black, horn-rimmed glasses, and he asked, "Did you get new glasses?"

I replied, "No!" my blood now boiling. "Do you mean to tell me that as I sit here, you don't notice anything different about me?"

The Lord so sweetly responded with this thought deep inside in my mind,
Did you ever think about what he's going through?

He said, "No! What?"

"I blew my hair off with the gas grill. I have almost no eyebrows. I'm bald where I used to have bangs, and my hair smells like it's singed."

He looked me in the eyes and said, "Oh," and went right back to his stir-fry.

I Wasn't Thinking

The girls were rolling on the floor. Now I was laughing because the girls were laughing, but then I realized, *Wait a minute. This isn't funny. It's ridiculous.* I was split right down the middle of half angry and half hurt. And I was totally frustrated.

I decided to go upstairs—loudly. I went into the bathroom and shut the door—firmly. There is nothing spiritual about shutting the door firmly, but that was the mood I was in. I was so upset, so hurt.

I looked up to God in total frustration and asked, "Did You notice what he said?"

And the Lord so sweetly responded with this thought deep inside in my mind, *Did you ever think about what he's going through?*

I thought, *I'm the injured one here,* and God kept on saying, "Did you ever think...."

No, I wasn't thinking.

Then clearly the Lord said, "You begin to pray for him with compassion, and don't stop until you see a change." And He added, "I am holding you responsible for his attitude. If you will pray for him, I will make it right."

I knew in my heart that this was a word from God. I was not sent into Richard's life to be a selfish, self-centered, me-first, me-only wife—especially in his time of great need. I was there to be a helpmeet, to help meet the needs he was having at that moment in his life.

When I married Richard, God really impressed on my heart that I was to "complete" Richard, never to "compete" with him.

Right then, at the dinner table, I was competing with him to see whose bad-day sob story was worse. I was sure mine was, so I wanted the attention for it. How ridiculous.

What God needed from me, as a good wife, was to fill in the gaps where Richard had need and complete him in prayer, in compassion, and do whatever it took to make him feel complete in a very difficult time in his life.

So when the Lord told me to pray for Richard and He would make it right, I immediately responded with, "Okay, Lord, You've got a deal."

His Moods Didn't Matter

During this time of intense pressure, God directed me to cancel luncheon outings with friends and stay home and pray for Richard. This was hard because what few times I went out for lunch were a much-welcomed relief from the "pressure cooker" atmosphere at home or at the office. But I knew God had a plan, so every day my mother and I would get together during that hour. We began to pray, and sometimes even weep, for my husband. I felt like we would literally pray heaven down.

Immediately the Lord stirred my heart, and I began to pour the love of God into Richard. His moods didn't matter. I did not care what he said. All I knew was that I was to sow seeds into his life, no matter what.

Whatever he said was perfect. When he said nothing, it was perfect silence. To me, everything about Richard was perfect.

My mom, my girls, and I began to feed him what he needed—the love of God, the peace of God, and the Word of God.

Richard was unusually, yet miraculously, transformed by being immersed in a baptism of joy.

I would look up to heaven and declare, "This man shall not die, but live and declare the works of the Lord. And this house is a house of joy, just as it has always been. Debt will not rob my joy."

A Baptism of Joy

Then one day, literally out of the clear blue, God performed a miracle for Richard, for our family, and for the university.

God told Richard that as he laughed, God would begin to move on the debt.

It was during these days that Richard received an invitation from one of the ORU regents, Pastor Karl Strader, to preach at his church in Lakeland, Florida.

During that journey Richard was unusually, yet miraculously, transformed by being immersed in a baptism of joy. Suddenly he experienced what the Word meant when it says, "The joy of the Lord is your strength" (Neh. 8:10).

The ulcer began to heal. The stress, the worry, the dread began to vanish, and it was one of those unexpected visits from the Holy Spirit.

God sent him to Lakeland a walking, talking dead man, and he came home a transformed man, filled with the joy of the Lord. He wasn't searching for it, but God sovereignly touched him. It was a back-to-the-future moment as God sent him back from Lakeland, restored to the man he was before all the stress and mess, and healed him to fulfill all that the future holds.

Financial Suicide?

The Lord also showed Richard that the mountain of the multimillion-dollar debt would begin to crumble as he experienced the joy of the Lord. God told Richard that as he laughed, God would begin to move on the debt.

Now that sounded ridiculous to my mind, but as Richard began to explain it to me, it made perfect sense. As Richard demonstrated that his faith and his trust were not in the debt but in God and in His Word, God would honor that faith and trust and begin to move against the debt.

God began to honor Richard's faith with one turn-around miracle after another.

God truly gave Richard insight into the Scripture, "The joy of the Lord is your strength." As he ignored the situation or circumstance and allowed the *joy of the Lord* to be his strength, Richard began to shine. And God began to shine through him.

If you are to be strong in the Lord and the power of His might, how can you be strong in the Lord without the joy of the Lord, which is your strength?

Richard allowed the Lord's peace and joy to be his strength. He had such an unwavering faith and trust in God that it really did not matter how deep the financial waters got. Richard trusted God. Period. God restored his joy, and the joy restored became a strength. A merry heart began to do Richard good, "like a medicine" (Prov. 17:22), and God began to honor Richard's faith with one turn-around miracle after another.

Richard began to tithe like never before and honor the Lord with corporate giving. Richard knew that the Bible states that tithing is the connector to receiving according to God's Word.

Malachi 3:10-11, Luke 6:38, and Galatians 6:7 are clear indicators that God established tithing as His method, and we are to honor God with tithes and offerings. This is serious to God and must be taken seriously. If we expect God to do His part and honor His Word, then we must do our part to honor His Word according to what it says concerning tithing.

I must tell you that in the middle of debt, tithing didn't go over well with everyone. One of the bankers protested, "You can't do that. It's financial suicide!"

But Richard clearly explained that as long as our bills were on time, the banker had no say in tithing. God had clearly spoken that this was a key to financial breakthrough, not financial suicide. It was in line with God's will and His Word, and we were tithing. Period.

You see, God's Word includes a plan—a formula—for rebuking the devourer (Mal. 3:10,11), and we knew God had spoken as a result of Richard's obedience.

The burden of debt began to shrink. It wasn't instant. (Oh, how we would have loved that.) It was a process, and the process was a tremendous learning experience.

And it wasn't a learning experience about debt or money. It was a learning experience about the faithfulness of a loving God who never leaves you nor forsakes you.

Lindsay's Reminders:

- The joy is not in falling but in *knowing* God.

- The Lord sees you as complete, perfect, made whole, and wanting nothing.

- God's Word is truth.

- God's Word never changes.

- Realize that the joy of the Lord is your strength.

- Regardless of the crisis, God has a plan for your deliverance.

In *every* situation, you can count it all joy because you know, that you know, that you know, that God is still on the throne. He will never leave you nor forsake you.

CHAPTER 3

Here's The Plan

Now you may say, "I'm smack-dab in the middle of a mess. So how on earth can I dig myself out?"

Yet when it seemed I was becoming overwhelmed in a tidal wave of tension and stress, the Holy Spirit led me to the Word and began to unveil a divine plan. And God's plan is a road that leads to victory.

When you go to the Word of God, one thing to remember is the Scripture in Isaiah 55:11 which says God's Word shall not return void. That means that the Word of God must produce something, and the thing God's Word produces and brings into effect is the will of God.

God's plan is a road that leads to victory.

Then to add even more power to it—literally adding unlimited power—God adds an incredible Scripture in Jeremiah 1:12 that says He watches over His Word to perform it.

First, God writes it. Then He gives us faith to believe it. Romans 12:3 says, "God hath dealt to every man the measure of faith."

Next, He teaches us how to activate that faith. Romans 10:17 says, "Faith cometh by hearing, and hearing by the word of God."

Then He commands us to use the faith we were given, for "faith without works is dead" (James 2:26).

Then God promises that His Word works because He said it can't come back void. And just to assure it, God said He watches over it to perform it. What blessed assurance.

Even though the particular Scriptures I want to share with you are powerful and can become life transforming, unless they are acted upon they might as well be fairy dust.

Even though they are truth and they are filled with power, they must be truth to *you* in order for them to be powerful to *you*.

Like water in a shower, it has all the properties to cleanse you. But until you actually get into the shower, turn on the water, and allow that water to start flowing over your head, it's not going to help you. It may be available to you, but you must avail yourself of it for it to be activated in your life.

God's Word is alive and full of power. God's Word is available. But even though it is available, you must in turn avail yourself of it to activate it and make it alive to you.

God's Word is alive and full of power, but in order to *change* you, it must be alive *to* you and alive *in* you to be alive *for* you.

> *Even though the particular Scriptures I want to share with you are powerful and can become life transforming, unless they are acted upon they might as well be fairy dust.*

Eight Vital Steps

I wish every person who is carrying the heaviness of stress and torment and doesn't know what to do could know how it feels to have the weight of distress lifted from their shoulders.

And in the natural, it may seem like just too much to carry, yet through the Word of God and activating your faith, anything is possible according to God's will.

1. Make the first move.

Take the heavy load that caused your shoulders to stoop and turn it over to Him.

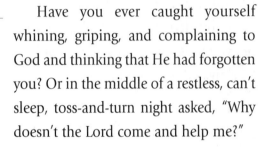

Have you ever caught yourself whining, griping, and complaining to God and thinking that He had forgotten you? Or in the middle of a restless, can't sleep, toss-and-turn night asked, "Why doesn't the Lord come and help me?"

But if we really understand God's nature and His Word, we learn that God has already done His part. He is waiting for us to do ours. Scripture is clear that you and I must initiate the action.

Jesus says, "Come unto me, all ye that labour and are heavy laden, and I will give you rest" (Matt. 11:28).

A sentence like this in English grammar is a command that carries an understood "you" at the beginning. "*You* come unto Me." The process begins with us.

2. Turn your problems over to God.

After taking that first step toward your heavenly Father, enter into fellowship and communion with Him. Then take the heavy load that caused your shoulders to stoop and turn it over to Him.

Go ahead! That's exactly what God's Word tells you to do. The psalmist wrote, "Cast thy burden upon the Lord, and he shall sustain thee" (Ps. 55:22).

Instead of dwelling on the problem, dwell on the Problem Solver.

So much of God's Word depends directly on our action, for as James 2:26 says, "Faith without works is dead." There must be a corresponding action of our faith to cause life to spark.

It's also a matter of our attitude being connected with our action. Some people wake up and say, "Good morning, Lord." Some wake up and say, "Good Lord! It's morning."

There's a lot to be said for our attitude, as it directly relates to the words we speak and the actions that follow.

Instead of dwelling on the problem, dwell on the Problem Solver. Consider starting the day with, "Good morning, Lord," and really mean it. Trust that God is well able to turn all things for good to them that love the Lord and are called according to His purpose. (Rom. 8:28.)

Establish your day from the moment you get up by asking God to renew your mind. God's Word says we can have the mind of Christ. Begin each day by casting all of your

God has given us a plan, a strategy, a way to take authority over Satan's attack.

cares (not anything that is your responsibility, but your cares) upon the Lord, for He cares for you. (1 Peter 5:7.)

3. Plug into the power.

The flame that burns on the campus of ORU is not an ordinary fire. It represents what happened on the Day of Pentecost when God sent His Holy Spirit to believers waiting in the Upper Room. "And there appeared unto them cloven tongues like as of fire, and it sat upon each of them" (Acts 2:3).

As a believer, Jesus promised that same power to you. He declared, "Ye shall receiver power, after that the Holy Ghost is come upon you" (Acts 1:8).

The enemy we are facing is fierce. Defeating him requires more than wishful thinking.

- Would you enter a conflict without total preparation?

- Would you go into battle without a strategy?

God has given us a plan, a strategy, a way to take authority over Satan's attack. To receive that plan, it's so easy to tap into God's power. And, according to His Word, that power source is found by tapping into the Holy Spirit, God's unlimited instruction plan.

The Bible says in Romans 8:26-27 that the Holy Spirit is always interceding before the throne of God. He is, in essence, praying a prayer twenty-four hours a day. And we have a right to join the Holy Spirit by praying in the Spirit, tapping into that prayer any time, anywhere. And it is ours for the asking.

Remember, the Holy Spirit is a gentleman. He is not going to force Himself against your will. You must *invite* Him to infuse you with His power.

4. Listen for a Word from heaven.

Whether you are engulfed in a crisis or not, you are daily bombarded with information—and much of it is not from heaven. You hear negative information from the media, on the job, from unbelievers, and from the devil himself. And oddly enough, you can even hear junk from people who call themselves Christians.

Consider distancing yourself from anything that would distract you from the Lord's plan for your life.

Starting this moment, I want to encourage you to guard yourself from garbage. Begin to pull yourself away from the noise of the world and turn your ears toward heaven. God's Word promises, "And thine ears shall hear a word behind thee, saying, This is the way, walk ye in it, when ye turn to the right hand, and when ye turn to the left" (Isa. 30:21).

What great news! The Lord Himself will tell you, "This is the way. Walk ye in it."

Don't fall prey to those who would tempt and entice you—the seducing spirits warned about by the apostle Paul. He wrote, "Now the Spirit speaketh expressly, that in the latter times some shall depart from the faith, giving heed to seducing spirits, and doctrines of devils; speaking lies in hypocrisy; having their conscience seared with a hot iron" (1 Tim. 4:1,2).

Consider distancing yourself from anything that would distract you from the Lord's plan for your life. If Satan is successful in snatching you from your obedience to God, he has begun a strategy to take you out from under the protection of God—and then you find yourself in deeper trouble.

Be on full alert. All through the Bible God warns, "Be careful. Take notice. Be aware. Guard yourself." I encourage you to be mindful of God speaking in that "still, small voice."

As you go through your daily routine, in all you do, be consciously listening for a Word from heaven.

5. Act on your faith.

I've heard many people say, "I'm believing that God is going to get me out of this predicament." And I am totally in favor of confessing what you believe. But let me encourage you to take it a step further, for you can have all the faith in the world, yet if you don't have corresponding action to your faith, that faith could die out. The Bible declares, "Faith without works is dead" (James 2:26).

So one very important point is recognizing that we *all* really do have faith.

Paul, writing to the believers in Rome, declared, "So then faith cometh by hearing, and hearing by the word of God" (Rom. 10:17).

The word for *hearing* in Hebrew is a picture word with three parts.

1. The information comes in.

2. The information is processed and understood.

3. Action is taken.

Unless we receive our marching orders from heaven, we could find ourselves marching in a parade that is headed straight into the jaws of death.

Now we can see here the meaning of the Scripture, "Faith without works is dead." It means faith without corresponding action has no ability to operate and be fulfilled.

God tells us that the source of our faith is the Word—and if we operate in faith, we will demonstrate it. Even God said He watches over His Word to perform it. He didn't just give us the Word. He goes on to watch over it and perform it, or bring it to action.

God tells us to be like Him. So if corresponding action is important to Him, it should be important to us also.

6. Let God direct your steps.

If you have ever observed the military, you know that orders come from the top and are filtered down and carried out by those down the chain of command.

As Christians, we could learn from that same truth. For unless we receive our marching orders from heaven, we could find ourselves marching in a parade that is headed straight into the jaws of death.

Long ago the prophet Jeremiah wrote, "O Lord, I know that the way of man is not in himself: it is not in man that walketh to direct his steps" (Jer. 10:23). And the psalmist declared, "The steps of a good man are ordered by the Lord: and he delighteth in his way" (Ps. 37:23).

I want to encourage you to consider a spiritual about-face. Rather than continuing on a road of your own choosing, pray and ask the Lord to guide you, lead you, and show you the pathway that He has prepared for you.

One thing I truly believe is that God certainly knows the best path that leads to heaven.

7. Praise God anyhow.

Regardless of the depth or the length of the valley, never stop praising the Lord. Why? Because it feels good? Sometimes I've reached places in certain circumstances where nothing felt good. In fact, there were days when I can honestly say I was just numb enough to feel nothing.

Faith and praise are not dependent on how or what we feel. Both are the exercise of an act of obedience to God's Word that allows us to receive His answers.

In my best interpretation of the Bible, the way to get God's response is to do things God's way. And one way He has established to exercise or demonstrate our faith is by the outward manifestation of our praise—regardless of

If I feel a million miles away from God, He can instantly find me in my praise.

how we feel or think about the circumstances. Then it becomes an act of obedience rather than an act of feelings.

And remember that God inhabits (or lives and dwells in) the praises of His people. "Thou art holy, O thou that inhabitest the praises of Israel" (Ps. 22:3).

I get great comfort and hope knowing that God lives and dwells in the praises of His people. I like the fact that He uses the word *inhabits*—lives and dwells in. That's a lot more comforting to hear than something like, "occasionally drops in" or "whenever."

I have a Bible-based assurance that God will find me in my praise. If I feel a million miles away from God, He can instantly find me in my praise. So I urge you:

It's not over until God says it's over, and God doesn't say it's over until we win.

- When your medical report contains bad news, praise Him.

- When a trusted friend has double-crossed you, praise Him.

- When your face is to the ground and your nose is pressed in the dirt, praise Him.

- In *all* situations, praise Him.

Now notice it clearly says *in* all situations. God never told us to praise Him

40

for all situations. That would be silly. You don't praise God for the devil beating the tar out of you. However, you praise God *in the midst* of all situations. Then God comes in with the power to beat the tar out of the devil in all situations.

As you raise your voice to the Lord, He then can arrive on the scene and command Satan to flee.

8. Never give up.

The Lord knew in advance that you would possibly become exhausted and fatigued on your journey. That's why His Word says, "Let us not be weary in well doing: for in due season we shall reap, if we faint not" (Gal. 6:9).

When will the answer come? In "due season"—in God's perfect timing.

Hang in there!

I like to confess that it's not over until God says it's over, and God doesn't say it's over until we win.

Whose Plan?

One key to graduating from stress to rest is to follow *God's* plan—not your own.

I'm sure you have met those who say, "It's my way or the highway." Personally, I don't want it to be my way. I want my life to go God's way, for I truly believe God's way *is* the *highway*. It's the successful way, for Proverbs 19:21 (NIV) says, "Many are the plans in a man's heart, but it is the Lord's purpose that prevails."

The word *prevail* here means "rise up or stand up."

Frankly, I'll take God's purpose over mine every time, for it's His purpose that will stand.

Lindsay's Reminders:

- Take the first step toward the Lord. Turn the problem over to God.

- Plug into the power of the Holy Spirit.

- Listen for a word from heaven. Act on your faith.

- Let God direct your steps.

- Praise the Lord in every situation. Never give up.

Starting today, believe for God's way in all that you do. For God is truly the only One who can say, "My way is the highway—the most high way from the Most High God for the rest of your life."

CHAPTER 4

"You're Full of It"

One hot Tulsa afternoon when our daughter Chloe was eight, she and a girlfriend had been playing in the swimming pool.

When they bounced into the house I told them, "Just like you are, run upstairs, jump into the shower, and rinse all that chlorine out of your hair and your bathing suits." Obediently, off they went.

Evidently, they hadn't finished playing yet for I was soon to discover their next project to entertain themselves. First, they turned on the shower, and then they plugged the drain and watched the water start rising. When it reached a certain level, they stuffed towels at the bottom of the door.

The goal of Chloe and her friend was to see how high the water would rise. If it got high enough, they planned to float. *What a great idea!* they thought.

I still shudder to think about what happened next. All of a sudden I heard Chloe bounding down the stairs and grabbing a handful of pans from the kitchen.

"What in the world are you doing? And where are you going with those pans?" I inquired, knowing full well in the pit of my stomach that Chloe Elisabeth Ann Roberts was up to something. And it wasn't something good.

I took a deep breath and gingerly opened the bathroom door and, oh my, what a sight. There was water, water everywhere.

"Mom, you don't want to know," replied Chloe sheepishly, "but you're going to have to punish me big time for this one." And, with the speed of a racehorse, she dashed upstairs.

I knew there was trouble brewing, and I went flying up the stairs behind her to the bathroom where I was greeted by a closed door.

"Chloe Elisabeth Ann Roberts, before I open this door do you have something you want to tell me first?"

"No," she said.

I took a deep breath and gingerly opened the bathroom door and, oh my, what a sight. There was water, water everywhere. And I mean everywhere.

Instantly, my first thought was concern for the rooms below. So I ran back downstairs to see what was seeping through. It was a flood like I had never seen before. I arrived just in time to see the water pouring through the ceiling and down into the light fixtures. When it drenched the electrical cords, the circuits shorted, and the lights sparked out.

"This Had Better Be Good"

I couldn't help thinking about the hilarious episode of *I Love Lucy,* when Lucy and Ethel were stuck in the shower and the water kept rising. That, however, was television. This was reality.

As I was assessing the situation, I said to my daughter, "Chloe, I'm going to give you one chance. Do you have

"Mommy, can you just tell me one thing. How do you learn to listen with your heart and not your head?"

anything you want to say to me before I ground you for the rest of your human existence?"

She took a deep breath and said, "Yes, Mother, I have just one thing I want to say."

"Think carefully, Chloe. You have only one chance. This had better be good," I responded.

"Well, my head was telling me to do this," Chloe said. "I thought it would be fun. But my heart was telling me no." Then she added, "And I listened to my head." Then she asked the question of all questions: "Mommy, can you just tell me one thing. How do you learn to listen with your heart and not your head?"

I melted right there. Chloe knew she had been wrong, but she sincerely wanted to learn—really discern—the difference in life's lessons of the head versus the heart.

And, obviously, these are lessons in decision-making that many of us struggle with every day of our lives. I knew right then that she was teachable, and we had a good place to start. When the Bible says in Proverbs 22:6, "Train up a child," I knew God meant it. I just didn't know life would be so interesting in the process.

Later, after the situation subsided, I was able to have a conversation with Chloe on the importance of listening with our heart rather than our head. I told her, "When you learn that lesson, you will be far ahead of most people."

Our head often tells us, "Go ahead. It will be a blast. There won't be consequences." Yet at the same time there is an inner voice from God that is sounding an alarm. You hear the warning, "Stop! Don't do it!"

God says we believe Him with our heart. The devil can mess with our head. But since God speaks in our heart and with the heart man believes, why not listen to our heart and believe that God knows best and is more than willing and well able to properly direct our path?

As Psalm 37:23 says, "The steps of a good man are ordered by the Lord: and he [God] delighteth in his way." They are ordered of God. If God orders and directs, then He also protects.

It's not what is stored in your head that keeps you from sinning—it is the Word hidden in your heart.

The Source

Your true thoughts are not birthed in your brain—the message is sent from deep within. The Bible states, "As he [a man] thinketh in his heart, so is he" (Prov. 23:7).

Thinking logically would cause you to say, "That must be a mistake. It should read, 'As a man thinketh in his *head,* so is he.'" But your head is the place you process information; your heart is where you believe. "For with the heart man believeth unto righteousness; and with the mouth confession is made unto salvation" (Rom. 10:10).

The apostle Paul counseled, "Be not conformed to this world: but be ye transformed by the *renewing of your mind,* that ye may prove what is that good, and acceptable, and perfect will of God" (Rom. 12:2).

How do we renew our mind? With Scripture. By hiding God's Word in the center of our heart—in the center of our belief system. In the process, God's everlasting Word works its way into our very being. As the psalmist declared, "Thy word have I hid in mine heart, that I might not sin against thee" (Ps. 119:11).

Most information goes in one ear and out the other— perhaps that's why God gave us two ears.

It's not what is stored in your head that keeps you from sinning—it is the Word hidden in your heart. "Out of the abundance of the heart the mouth speaketh" (Matt. 12:34). And, "Death and life are in the power of the tongue" (Prov. 18:21).

If we realize how very powerful our tongue is—how powerfully creative our words are to create a good or bad situation—we become very aware of what we say. When we are aware of how important our creative words are, we become very careful of what words we choose to hide in our heart.

When the words in our heart line up with the Word of God, and God watches over His Word to perform it, we can set up a system, an atmosphere, to watch God work. Then we're acting out His will rather than our will for our lives.

Your Filtering System

God has given us the power to choose—the option to decide what to keep and what to discard. Most information goes in one ear and out the other—perhaps that's why God gave us two ears. In between, however, is what I call the devil's playground—the mind. Is it any wonder that Romans 12:2 says to renew our mind daily with the Word of God.

Your head contains an amazing filtering system. Every concept or piece of data that enters your mind can be calculated, analyzed, kept, or rejected. You can also make the decision to send that message directly to your heart and soul.

Whose Voice?

As clear as a bell, I heard this sweet voice of the Lord say, "I talk like I write, and I write like I talk."

You would think people would know the difference between the voice of their best friend and the voice of their worst enemy, yet they don't.

So many times I've heard the question, "Is this God or is it the devil speaking?" You know, I used to want to give some brilliant theological answer, but the best response to that statement I've ever heard was when my mother said to me, "How can you not know the voice of your best friend from the voice of your worst enemy?"

As I thought of what a great statement that was, I heard that sweet, still, small voice of the Holy Spirit saying, "It's easy to tell the difference."

I thought, *God, what are You trying to show me here?*

As clear as a bell, I heard this sweet voice of the Lord say, "I talk like I write, and I write like I talk."

Immediately I realized God said in Malachi 3:6, "I am the Lord, I change not." God is very consistent. He can speak to us any way He chooses—from an impression in our heart, from the written Word, the spoken Word, or through godly instruction. But no matter the means of communication, God's Word is still the same. It's always for our good. He talks like He writes, and He writes like He talks.

The best way I know to recognize the unmistakable voice of the Lord is really quite simple: Spend time—enormous amounts of time—in His presence. I'm certainly not against a quick, "Help me, Lord!" prayer to get you through an immediate situation, but there is nothing to compare with continually staying on your face before the Lord in fellowship and communion with Him and His Word.

A mind-driven person is going to waver, but a heart-driven believer can rely on an unwavering, unchanging, almighty God.

I believe it will bring some answers to the question, "Is this God's voice?" Remember, He talks like He writes, and He writes like He talks.

Mind Games

Why is the devil constantly playing mind games with us?

I believe Satan's goal is to confuse your thinking so you won't have clear information to believe in your heart. He knows that a mind-driven person is going to waver, but a heart-driven believer can rely on an unwavering, unchanging, almighty God.

Jesus declared, "Out of the abundance of the heart the mouth speaketh" (Matt. 12:34). Amazing! The very words you speak are not being formed in your mind—they flow directly from your heart.

Lindsay's Reminders:

- Your true thoughts stem from the heart.

- Belief wins from within.

- Your mind is renewed through God's Word.

- Learn to recognize God's voice.

- What is on the inside will eventually surface.

Begin to establish a routine of spending quality time with the Word of God. Learn the familiar sound of God's still, small voice. Remember, God talks like He writes, and He writes like He talks.

If you fill your heart with peace—if you fill your soul with joy, if you fill your life with the Word—it can bring health and healing to you.

Proverbs 4:20-23 says, "My son, attend to my words; incline thine ear unto my sayings. Let them not depart from thine eyes; keep them in the midst of thine heart. For they are life unto those that find them, and health to all their flesh. Keep thy heart with all diligence; for out of it are the issues of life."

"Life and health to your flesh." Now doesn't that sound like something we would all like to have? Well, God's formula for achieving this is simple—give attention, or pay attention, to His Word, for this Scripture declares that its power begins to generate life and health to those who obey that Word.

CHAPTER 5

Speak to Your Stress

If someone walked up to you and said, "You're full of it!" whether or not that would be a compliment would depend on what you are full of. What is on the inside will make itself known.

- If you are filled with anger, what will emerge? Anger.

- If you are filled with frustration, what will surface? Frustration.

- If you are filled with tension and stress, what will come out? Tension and stress.

- If you are filled with the love of God, what do you think will come pouring out? The love of God.

The Big Lemon Question

What do you get when you squeeze a lemon? You get whatever is on the inside. The only thing that can come out is what's on the inside. You can squeeze and squeeze as hard as you possibly can, but you will never get orange juice.

> *What do you get when you're squeezed? You get whatever it is that you've put on the inside.*

So the next question is, What do you get when you're squeezed? You get whatever it is that you've put on the inside.

And I firmly believe that as long as we're breathing, we will be pressed on every angle. Therefore, what you're made of is eventually going to come out.

If you place nothing inside, you are not empty. *You're just full of nothing.* And guess what will come out when you are squeezed? You are right. Nothing.

Again, let me ask. What are you full of?

Speak to Your Stress

When God created this earth, He spoke the words, "Light be!" and *light was.* It was that simple. The Lord spoke this world into existence with His words. Today He blesses His children with the same awesome creative power of the spoken Word.

Through our faith in God's authority and as Christians, we have the ability to speak life into situations instead of death. Scripture declares, "Death and life are in the power of the tongue: and they that love it shall eat the fruit thereof" (Prov. 18:21).

We also can stand on God's promise and "call those things which be not as though they were" (Rom. 4:17).

As we begin to operate in faith, by faith, and through faith, we not only can speak to our stress, but we also can receive great strength. We can become a powerhouse for the kingdom of God.

Life and Health

The key to a triumphant life is to meet God's prerequisites. Here is what God says: "My son, attend to my words; incline thine ear unto my sayings. Let them not depart from thine eyes; keep them in the midst of thine heart" (Prov. 4:20,21). In those verses the Lord involves the totality of our senses and emotion.

- Speech—"Attend to my words."

- Hearing—"Incline thine ear unto my sayings."

- Sight—"Let them not depart from thine eyes."

- Heart—"Keep them in the midst of thine heart."

These elements allow the Word to saturate us, and they are essential to our life and health. "For they are life unto those that find them, and health to all their flesh. Keep thy heart with all diligence; for out of it are the issues of life" (Prov. 4:22,23).

How many miraculous unanswered prayers and empty words must pass by God's ears each day when, in fact, it's faith in God, faith in His Word, and confession of the Word that trigger God's responses.

What you place in your heart and speak with your lips can generate an environment for either life or death, health or disease.

Watch Your Words

Studies have shown that on an average day, women speak more than twice as many words as men. Let's face it. We love to talk.

And really, men and women are guilty at times of saying things they don't really mean. And instead of saying, "Get thee behind me, Satan. You cannot prevail," we catch ourselves saying things like, "It's going to be a mess!" Or, "Oh, I wish I were dead." Or, "I'm trying to catch a cold."

Now I want you to close your eyes and get a very clear mental picture of this one. There you are outside running as fast as you can, and doing what? Trying to catch a cold. There it goes, only steps ahead of you at top speed—the nose, the sinus drainage, the virus, the whole thing—tissues flying everywhere. And there you are, running like a champion—full speed, arms going, legs stretched, sweat flying—because you're trying to catch a cold.

I sometimes wonder if God sits in heaven and says, "For heaven's sake, slow down. Don't catch it."

How many miraculous unanswered prayers and empty words must pass by God's ears each day when, in fact, it's faith in God, faith in His Word, and confession of the Word that trigger God's responses. Yet even though we have a very clear-cut formula in Proverbs 4:20-23, our job isn't just to read it. We must read it, confess it, believe it by faith, and act on it.

Instead of people believing they can have what they say, many do just the opposite—they simply say what they already have.

Otherwise, according to the Bible, how can God perform it? For Jeremiah 1:12 says God watches over *His word* to perform it. He doesn't watch over our bad-hair or bad-faith days, or bad-anything else. Jeremiah 1:12 clearly says He watches over His Word to perform it.

Nothing but the Truth

God's Word directs us to be careful. Our words are powerful, and what we say can come to pass. However, instead of people believing they can have what they say, many do just the opposite—they simply say what they already *have.*

- "I'm broke."

- "I'm sick."

- "I can't."

- "I won't."

- "I never will."

I said to a young woman, "Start claiming your promise!"

"Well, I wouldn't be telling the truth," she responded.

"No," I told her. "You would be lining up your words with the Word of God."

"Well, what if I have cancer?" she asked,

"That may be the medical report—and a fact," I replied, "but here is the truth. God said, 'I am the Lord that healeth thee'" (Ex. 15:26).

Both fact and truth may be reports that exist, and they may be completely different. So you must declare by your words that you believe the truth found in the Word of God. Then command the facts to line up with the truth, line up with the Word of God. Isaiah 53:1 says, "Whose report shall you believe?"

Both truth and fact may exist. But begin to declare that you choose by faith to believe the report of the Lord and confess it over and over, day after day.

Father Really Does Know Best

God declares, "I call heaven and earth to record this day against you, that I have set before you life and death, blessing and cursing: therefore choose life, that both thou and thy seed may live" (Deut. 30:19).

Now when you read that verse, don't think that God is mad, asking heaven and earth to investigate you so He can zap you into the pits of hell. No. God simply says everything

The words that spring from your heart and out of your mouth have the authority of heaven.

will be recorded—and used according to what you do and say.

This gives God a record so He has the opportunity to say, in essence, "There's proof. Look at that faith. They are speaking life, believing life, and choosing life."

The heavenly Father, through His Word, tells you to "choose life so that you and your descendants may live." He says, "I am watching. I have heaven and earth to stand as My witness."

God is on record honoring our words. It's true. What we believe, confess, and speak will come to pass.

It's like God says to the Holy Spirit, "What did she say to her husband this morning, or to her children? What did she say that I am obligated to perform?"

The words that spring from your heart and out of your mouth have the authority of heaven. God honors them, whether they speak encouragement or sorrow, comfort or distress, life or death.

His witnesses include angels, the Holy Spirit, the Lord Jesus Christ, and God Himself. Even the earth becomes a witness of your words. Then, if Satan tries to rear his ugly head and say, "Oh, no!" God can say, "Oh, yes! By faith, through faith, and in faith my child has declared this."

Now don't miss that. This is not the guilt trap catchall for Satan to say you didn't get your prayers answered because you didn't have any faith or enough faith. Remember, God is still God. He's sovereign. He makes sovereign decisions in some cases that we may never understand until we get to heaven.

Faith isn't our manipulating God to do what we say, when we say it—or forget God. And our faith is not to boast that we always get what we want. That would be a controlling spirit like witchcraft. And it's certainly not to be used as faith in our faith. That would really be more like pride.

True faith is letting God be God and trusting that He is the One who truly knows and sees everything. His ways are higher than our ways. His thoughts are higher than our thoughts. He knows the beginning from the end. And Father really does know best.

What About Your Friends?

If someone asked you, "Do you choose life or death?" you'd probably respond, "That's ridiculous. I choose life."

Even if we might not deliberately and outwardly choose death, sometimes we choose things that do not breathe life

Even tiny distractions can lead to destruction.

into our situations. Jesus refers to Himself as a friend who sticks closer than a brother. (Prov. 18:24.) He made a deliberate point to show us the importance of choosing friends who bring life to us and not death.

Life is not just breathing, as in existence, but it is also the quality of that existence. The atmosphere created in that existence can be added to or taken away from by the company we keep. And Jesus was careful to explain the value of those we keep close to us.

Our friends create an atmosphere that brings something to our situation. They add something to the party. The question is, What are they bringing? Are they creating an atmosphere that leads to a pity party or a spiritual atmosphere that lifts you up rather than pulls you down?

I'm reminded of the saying, "We're known by the company we keep." So let's take a look at the atmosphere.

Are your friends taking you down the path that will bring blessing to your home, marriage, family, and finances? Or are they just taking up valuable time and space in your life?

In order to choose life, we must embrace the things that *generate* life—not those that bring distraction, dissension, and conflict.

Even tiny distractions can lead to destruction. As my mother always says, "It's not the mile walk that will kill you; it's the pebble in your shoe." Sometimes it's the tiny little things we ignore that, when added into the whole picture, lead to devastation. And yet we ignore them because they seem too insignificant at the time.

One trap I believe we must be very careful not to fall into is the easy access "gospel according to opinion."

But in order to de-stress, even little things need to line up with the Word of God. Remember, it's the little foxes that spoil the vine. (Song 2:15.)

Go to the Throne, Not the Phone

The power of agreement is one of God's plans, yet we need to be very careful when choosing a prayer partner—someone we believe will help spark our faith—because the power of agreement works. Whether negative or positive, it can still work. Sometimes just the opposite of faith happens. Some people can ignite your fear. One trap I believe we must be very careful not to fall into is the easy access "gospel according to opinion." What does my girlfriend think? Or, What does "he said, she said" think?

Sadly, many go to the phone before they go to the throne trying to find someone to agree with their opinion.

We have certainly seen that it doesn't take long to find a sympathetic ear—one who will wallow in the mud with you. Whining. Griping. Complaining.

That's why I always say to beware of what I call the "granola bar" friends—the fruits, the flakes, and the nuts. They'll agree with you on anything. They preach a very convincing gospel according to opinion. Yet, the best friend anyone could ever have is the one who will direct you straight to the throne of God.

What you stop

on earth is

stopped in heaven,

and what you

permit on earth is

permitted in heaven.

It's God's Commitment

Do you realize that your words have the kind of creative power that can stop Satan in his tracks? They can *bind* him.

Jesus said, "Verily I say unto you, Whatsoever ye shall bind on earth shall be bound in heaven; and whatsoever ye shall loose on earth shall be loosed in heaven. Again I say unto you, That if two of you shall agree on earth as touching any thing that they shall ask, it shall be done for them of my Father which is in heaven" (Matt. 18:18,19).

The word *verily* has been translated as "Assuredly, I say to you." The Lord is saying, "I mean it. I swear by it. I promise."

God has given you a commitment. What you stop on earth is stopped in heaven, and what you permit on earth is permitted in heaven.

Have you ever thought about the Scriptures that describe your authority over Satan? Isn't that what Jesus is asking you to do in those verses? One question to consider is whether or not you are obeying God's Word. Are you releasing or stopping the blessings of God?

What Do You Allow?

I remember a time when I felt a check in my spirit concerning a young lady one of my daughters was associating with. It was really bugging me. Yet I allowed some things to happen because I thought, *Don't rock the boat.*

That was a serious mistake.

A few days later I noticed an action and a reaction in my daughter that was like a mirror image of this person.

Then I heard the unmistakable voice of the Lord reminding me, "What you allow you go into agreement with."

I said, "That's it. It stops today." I decided, at the risk of hurting my daughter, that I would not permit that association any longer.

I realized that a short-term hurt would be a long-term benefit, no matter how difficult the process.

In the midst of that situation, God again brought the Word before me—"If two of you shall agree on earth as touching any thing that they shall ask, it shall be done for them of my Father which is in heaven" (Matt. 18:19).

If the giant you face is tension, anxiety, or stress, don't speak about it; speak to it.

The verse does not say whether what we agree on is good, bad, or indifferent. *Whatever* we agree upon will be done by God.

What you agree to, you are *bound* to—including the consequences.

Talk to Your Mountain

Jesus didn't tell us to talk *about* the mountain we face. He commanded that we talk *to* our mountain. He declared, "If ye have faith as a grain of mustard seed, ye shall say unto this mountain, Remove hence to yonder place; and it shall remove: and nothing shall be impossible unto you"

(Matt. 17:20). And, "If ye shall say unto this mountain, Be thou removed, and be thou cast into the sea; it shall be done" (Matt. 21:21).

If the giant you face is tension, anxiety, or stress, don't speak *about* it; speak *to* it. According to the will and the Word of God, you have a Bible right to bind it in Jesus' name.

Lindsay's Reminders:

- You can speak life or death to your situation.

- Let the Word of God concerning your situation saturate every part of you.

- Proclaim God's truth.

- Always choose life.

- Exercise the power of agreement.

- Your words can bind Satan.

- Talk *to* your mountain, not *about* it.

If you fill your heart with peace, it can calm every storm. If you fill your soul with joy, it can flow like a river. If you fill your life with the Word, it can bring health and healing.

CHAPTER 6

There's a Reward Coming

I remember a day when Olivia and Chloe were preparing for a spelling test. During their practice exam at home, Chloe got ten out of ten, and Olivia got three out of ten. Chloe was thrilled, and Olivia was grateful for the three right answers.

For this particular test, they were learning to spell the *"e-a"* words—like *treasure.*

Olivia was struggling with the concept; the sounds and the letters didn't seem to connect. So we kept trying.

We were sitting around the dining room table when we got the idea that every time Olivia came to an e-a she should do a little dance. G-R-E-A-T.

It was absolutely perfect for her personality.

Well, Olivia came home on Friday and shocked us with a perfect spelling paper—ten out of ten. Chloe also had a perfect score.

Delighted, I asked Olivia, "How did you do it?"

She said, "Every time I got to an *e-a*, I saw myself dancing the cha-cha."

That was her new kind of word association—and it worked.

"*Yes, Yes, Yes!*"

When we arrived home, Richard was already upstairs. We couldn't wait to tell our spelling news. I said, "Richard, you've got to hear this. Olivia has something to tell you."

"What's the news?" Richard called down.

"Dad, I got a ten out of ten on my spelling test!" replied Olivia. And she started dancing around.

Richard seized the moment and added his own excitement. He did a little Elvis routine. Both girls were jumping and shouting for joy.

"Yes, yes, yes! Good job!" Richard shouted from up above.

Olivia was hollering, "I did it! I did it!"

"This deserves a treat," said Richard. He pulled out his wallet and grabbed a five-dollar bill, which was her entire week's allowance.

"What are you doing?" I wanted to know.

"I have to reward her," he said tossing the bill in her direction. It floated down the stairs into Olivia's waiting hands. He also leaned over the balcony from above and sent the same to Chloe for her perfect paper. And we all danced and rejoiced, first for Olivia's diligence and then for her father's reward.

What a fun time we had.

The Rewarder

Now this may sound strange to some, but at that moment I saw a picture of God wearing a white robe in heaven. He was jumping up and down saying, "Yes! Yes! Amen!"

The Scripture came before me, "For all the promises of God in him are yea, and in him Amen" (2 Cor. 1:20).

Just as Richard was compelled to send the reward down, the Lord has the same desire. The Word says that "he is a rewarder of them that diligently seek him" (Heb. 11:6). And Psalm 35:27 says that God takes pleasure in the prosperity of His children.

Just as it pleased Richard to reward two of his girls, so God takes great pleasure in rewarding us. There was such joy in the diligence, the accomplishment, and in the reward— both from the giver and the receivers.

If worthiness were ever an issue with God, Jesus would never have come to earth and died for our sins.

Well, according to the Word, God delights in our diligence, in His giving the reward, and in our receiving rewards as well. The Lord loves to honor our perseverance. And that should be enough to make us all dance and shout.

You Are Worthy

God is ready to pour out His blessings from heaven, yet many say, "I'm not worthy of His favor." But it's not a matter of our worthiness. It's simply a matter of God's goodness. Jesus is the worthy One—worthy of our praise, love, honor, and worship.

If worthiness were ever an issue with God, Jesus would never have come to earth and died for our sins. He didn't come for our worthiness. In fact, He came so we could be forgiven. You don't need forgiveness if you are already perfect and worthy. Forgiveness is a gift we didn't earn. So worthiness never seemed to be an issue.

God's gifts are not intended to enrich Satan's kingdom. He sent Jesus to earth "that he might destroy the works of the devil" (1 John 3:8).

Poverty, stress, worry, and sickness—they are all works of Satan. And Jesus came to set us free. "(He) went about doing good, and healing all that were oppressed of the devil; for God was with him" (Acts 10:38). So, again, it's not our worthiness that counts; it's His godliness.

Words From the Prophet

In the Old Testament there is a marvelous story of a Shunammite woman who showed great kindness to Elisha.

As a way of saying thanks the prophet asked, "What can I do for you?" When he was informed that the woman did not have a child he said, "By the same time next year, you're going to have a son." (2 Kings 4:16.)

It happened. Scripture records that "the woman conceived, and bare a son at that season that Elisha had said unto her" (v. 17).

As the story continues, the child grew up and was working with his father in the fields when, unexpectedly, the boy screamed, "My head! My head!"

The father asked that the son be carried to his mother where he died.

She Wouldn't Let Go

The woman immediately asked her husband for a mule and a helper, "that I may run to the man of God" (v. 22).

She didn't yell. She didn't panic or fall apart. She simply decided to get to the prophet.

The woman's son was already dead, yet to every person around her she said, "It is well" (v. 23 NKJV). Not one negative word came out of the Shunammite woman's mouth.

As she approached Mount Carmel, Elisha saw her coming and said to Gehazi, his servant, "Run now, I pray thee, to meet her, and say unto her, Is it well with thee? is it well with thy husband? is it well with the child? And she answered, It is well" (v. 26).

When she reached Elisha, "she caught him by the feet" (v. 27 NKJV) and wouldn't let go. She said, "I won't turn loose until you come and help me!"

What determination.

It was faith, obedience to God, and diligence that brought the miracle.

The Miracle

Elisha went to the woman's house and "lay upon the child, and put his mouth upon his mouth, and his eyes upon his eyes, and his hands upon his hands: and he stretched himself upon the child; and the flesh of the child waxed warm" (v. 34).

What happened next? "The child sneezed seven times, and the child opened his eyes" (v. 35).

It was faith, obedience to God, and diligence that brought the miracle. The Word says, "If thou wilt diligently hearken to the voice of the Lord thy God, and wilt do that which is right in his sight, and wilt give ear to his commandments, and keep all his statutes, I will put none of these diseases upon thee, which I have brought upon the Egyptians: for I am the Lord that healeth thee" (Ex. 15:26).

Strong in the Lord

Do you realize it's okay to fight with your faith—to stand and be strong?

All throughout the Bible, men and women demonstrated amazing authority and persistence. And today we too can be "strong in the Lord, and in the power of his might" (Eph. 6:10).

I am grateful that I have a husband and a covering. But I also know that God has placed a strength in me—in all of us. And He has given us this assurance: "I will never leave thee, nor forsake thee" (Heb. 13:5).

The Lord gives us the ability to use His Word, His will, and His power to defeat the enemy.

Getting the Message

The Lord also exercises persistence. He keeps dealing with us until we get the message.

Four separate times the Bible declares, "The just shall live by faith" (Rom. 1:17; Hab. 2:4; Gal. 3:11; Heb. 10:38).

Sometimes I think it was repeated just for me.

That's okay, because often that's what it takes to get through to me. It is through repetition that the Lord teaches us how to obtain the character and the nature of God.

"Keep Praying, Mom!"

When Jordan was about three years old, we owned a two-door car, and she was scrambling into the backseat. I pulled the lever and folded the seat forward to let her in.

As she was getting ready to put on her seatbelt, I lifted the seat back and sat down, not realizing that Jordan's little foot was caught in the fold of the seat.

She screamed at the top of her lungs, and instantly I realized what I had done. Almost in a frenzy, I scrambled to get off the seat and get her foot out.

In the sweetest voice, Jordan cried, "Pray, Mom, pray!"

So I started to pray while strapping her back into the seatbelt, and off we went down the road.

We hadn't driven a block when Jordan said, "Pray again, Mom!"

This time I prayed a much different prayer. Yet it wasn't long until she said, "Don't stop! Keep praying, Mom!"

I quoted several verses and said, "Be healed in Jesus' name."

> *Seeking God isn't like pressing a button on the microwave.*

After several blocks of this same conversation and prayer and more conversation and prayer, I finally said, "How many times do you want me to pray?"

And with the most serious, determined conviction she said, "Mom, pray until the pain stops." And, believe me, I did. What a valuable lesson in persistence we can learn if we continue to pray "until the pain stops."

Don't Give Up

Seeking God isn't like pressing a button on the microwave. Diligence means to do it, and do it, and *keep on* doing it until your breakthrough comes. Pray, and don't stop until you receive the answer.

Sometimes I think Satan gets tired of hearing my voice. I nag and badger him with every fiber of my being. I read the Word to him and declare, "It is written!" Not only does it remind me of the Word, but it also reminds the devil.

Stand firm on the promises of God. Begin to pray, "Father, in the name of Jesus, I thank You for this opportunity. I thank You, Father God, that You are a God of miracles. And I thank

You, Lord, that every word that comes out of my mouth means 'yes' and 'amen' to the glory of God."

Lindsay's Reminders:

- God rewards diligence.

- Speak words of faith.

- Believe for your miracle, and don't let go.

- Be strong in the Lord.

- Never ever give up.

Keep praying. Keep believing. Keep expecting that God's reward is on the way, according to Galatians 6:7-9:

Be not deceived; God is not mocked: for whatsoever a man soweth, that shall he also reap. For he that soweth to his flesh shall of the flesh reap corruption; but he that soweth to the Spirit shall of the Spirit reap life everlasting.

CHAPTER 7

From Blaming to Blessing

When the headaches of life are throbbing and you are about to explode, what is your response?

- Many blame the circumstances.

- Some blame their childhood.

- Others blame their family or friends.

- Sadly, many blame God.

When stress knocks at your door—as it certainly will try—there's a surefire way to begin an escape: *Stop blaming and start blessing.*

When stress knocks at your door— as it certainly will try—there's a surefire way to begin an escape: Stop blaming and start blessing.

Turn your attention to heaven and start blessing God. Remember, Psalm 22:3 says God inhabits—lives and dwells in—the praises of His people. Instead of saying something that turns people away or turns God away, why not consider blessing and praising God and drawing Him into the situation rather than pushing Him away?

Amazing Benefits

How do you replace tension, fear, and anguish with redemption, love, and mercy? Follow the plan of the psalmist:

> *Bless the Lord, O my soul, and forget not all his benefits: Who forgiveth all thine iniquities; who healeth all thy diseases; Who redeemeth thy life from destruction; who crowneth thee with loving-kindness and tender mercies; Who satisfieth thy mouth with good things; so that thy youth is renewed like the eagle's.*

PSALM 103:2-5

In verse 1 the psalmist said, "Bless the Lord." Then he repeated it again, "Bless the Lord." This sentence begins with what's called in English grammar an "understood you." The "you" tells who is to do the action. In other words, *You* bless the Lord." Your job is to bless the Lord over and over. And when *all* that is within you begins to bless His holy name, then you are entitled to all the benefits.

It's amazing how simple God made our part. All we have to do to receive His benefits is bless the Lord with our entire being. His part is to forgive our iniquities, to heal our diseases, to redeem our lives from destruction, to crown us with loving-kindness and tender mercies, and to renew our youth like the eagle's. It sure seems like we've got the easier part of this equation. However, it's very clear that we do have a job. And our job is to bless the Lord.

- Your iniquities can be forgiven.

- Your diseases can be healed.

- Your life can be redeemed from destruction.

- You can be crowned with love, kindness, and mercy.

- You can be satisfied with good things.

- Your youth is designed to be renewed like the eagle's.

But these results are possible because of exercising the first requirement: "Bless the Lord."

Soul and Spirit

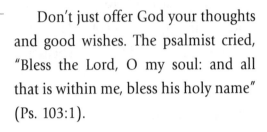

When you got up this morning, did you get up saying, "Good morning, Lord," or, "Good Lord, it's morning!"?

Don't just offer God your thoughts and good wishes. The psalmist cried, "Bless the Lord, O my soul: and all that is within me, bless his holy name" (Ps. 103:1).

Do you reach out to the Lord with *all* that is within you? Including your mouth?

Spiritually, we have a "spirit man" and a "soul man." Your spirit man is your relationship with God, and when you are born again that part is taken care of concerning eternity and making heaven your permanent home.

However, you live in a real world with a fleshly body that includes your soul. And your soul man is comprised of your mind, your will, and your emotions.

When you got up this morning, did you get up saying, "Good morning, Lord," or, "Good Lord, it's morning!"? Did your spirit man begin to praise and bless the Lord?

- Did you bless the Lord with your mind today?

- Did you bless the Lord with your will today?

- Did you bless the Lord with your emotions today?

Or did you just get up, brush your teeth, make coffee, and start the day? Well, if the answer is "just got up," how can we expect the Lord to do His part when we haven't done our part?

But if we get up and obey God's Word according to Psalm 103:1-5 and bless the Lord with *all* that is within us, then the combined power of these three elements—our minds, our wills, our emotions—can result in God releasing His marvelous benefits.

What a Fragrance

When you honor the Lord, you can sense the entire environment changing.

I remember standing in the cosmetic department of a store as a woman was giving a product demonstration on how to put on perfume.

She said, "Always buy spray perfume. Here's why. If you dab it on you, it's concentrated in one spot and overwhelming, and that's not good. It ruins the way the perfume was intended to smell."

"Your words are like perfume. You spray them into the atmosphere, walk through them, and carry them around with you all day long."

87

Then she said, "Here is how it is supposed to be applied." She extended the perfume in front of her as far as her hand could reach and said, "Give it a spray. Then walk into the perfume, and the mist goes all over you."

Immediately, the Lord gave me a wonderful thought. He said, "Your words are like perfume. You spray them into the atmosphere, walk through them, and carry them around with you all day long." And He said, "Just like that perfume, your words have a certain fragrance." In fact, the Bible says our words go up as a fragrance in the very nostrils of God. Then He basks in the essence of our words throughout the day.

Also, Psalm 19:14 says, "Let the words of my mouth, and the meditation of my heart, be acceptable in thy sight, O Lord, my strength, and my redeemer."

For God to be our strength and our Redeemer, I believe it's vital that the words of our mouths line up with God's Word and are a pleasing fragrance before His throne.

So a good question to ask yourself is this: Are your words a sweet-smelling aroma in the nostrils of God? If so, praise God; and if not, ask the Father to touch your heart with a way to line up your words with His Word.

A Prospering Soul

When you bless the Lord, everything about your life can begin to prosper. When God said, "Beloved, I wish above all things that thou mayest prosper and be in health, even as thy soul prospereth" (3 John 2), He was indicating His wish for your life to be filled with goodness, blessing, and prosperity in all areas.

Those words were written as a greeting, much like a person saying, "I hope you are doing well!"

However, if you tell someone, "I desire that you do as well as your soul is doing," that may not be the prayer they want to hear. It depends on whether or not they are serving and blessing the Lord with their soul. Psalm 103:1-2 says, "Bless the Lord, O my soul," which means bless the Lord with your mind, your will, and your emotions.

How you determine to bless the Lord with your soul leads you into the next part of that Scripture, which tells you the "benefits." The psalmist said, "Now don't forget the benefits." The Lord forgives your iniquities, heals your diseases, redeems your life from destruction, and satisfies your mouth with such good things that your youth is renewed like the eagle's. What benefits you receive when you bless the Lord with your soul, your mind, your will, and your emotions.

Blessing the Lord establishes the mark.

Now looking back at 3 John 2, we learn that the same proportional measure that our soul (mind, will, and emotions) prospers plays an important part as to what level the "prosper and be in health" will operate. As we determine the level we prosper in our soul, we also see the thermostat or the level we reach to prosper and be in health in every other area of life.

This leads me to believe that blessing the Lord with our soul—carefully establishing the level in God that we discipline our mind, will, and emotions—is vitally important to other areas of our life. And, in a sense, it determines the level we will achieve in the areas of prosperity and being in health.

Blessing the Lord establishes the mark. All other areas to prosper and be in health will hit that same level as a target point and will only go as high or to the same level that we prosper in our soul.

In the book of 3 John, the disciple knew he was writing to a believer whose soul was in a right relationship with Jesus Christ. He was greeting a person who was prospering in his mind, his will, and his emotions.

We can *know* that our soul is thriving when we continually pray, "Let the words of my mouth, and the meditation of my heart, be acceptable in thy sight, O Lord, my strength, and my redeemer" (Ps. 19:14).

One translation for the word *acceptable* is "a delight."

Once again, when our words and prayers become a delight in the sight of God, He becomes our strength and our Redeemer.

"If My People..."

In law school, we learned the importance of "if-then" suppositions. If *this* happens, then *this* will happen. And the opposite is also true. If this *does not* happen, then this *will not* happen.

God's Word is filled with truth based on the same principle.

So often we pray that God will do His part, yet we are reluctant to do ours.

> *If my people, which are called by my name, shall humble them-selves, and pray, and seek my face, and turn from their wicked ways; then will I hear from heaven, and will forgive their sin, and will heal their land.*
>
> 2 CHRONICLES 7:14

> *If thou shalt confess with thy mouth the Lord Jesus, and shalt believe in thine heart that God hath raised him from the dead, thou shalt be saved.*
>
> ROMANS 10:9

Give, and it shall be given unto you.

Luke 6:38

So often we pray that God will do *His* part, yet we are reluctant to do ours. That's not the divine arrangement.

The Word says, "Delight thyself also in the Lord; and he shall give thee the desires of thine heart" (Ps. 37:4). We need to delight ourselves in the Lord first *and* do our part. *Then* God can do His part and give us the desires of our hearts.

Something Good

God gave us a promise. He said He would keep every pledge He makes to us because the Bible records, "Not a word failed of any good thing which the Lord had spoken to the house of Israel. All came to pass" (Josh. 21:45 NKJV).

In fact, Jeremiah 1:12 says God watches over His Word to perform it. How amazing! First God writes it, speaks it, and then keeps close watch over each word to perform it when we do our part and obey it and stretch forth in faith to believe it.

- What did God speak? *Words.*

- What did His words say? *Good things.*

- What was the result? *They all came to pass.*

One of the reasons we called our live daily television program, *Something Good Tonight—THE HOUR OF HEALING,* was simple. There is certainly enough evil taking place in our world. But in spite of the evil plan of Satan, the Lord promises "something good." For decades my father-in-law has spoken the phrase, "Something good is going to happen to you." In fact, he has received letters actually written to "The Something Good Man." Well, the original "Something Good Man" was Jesus.

God's Word says in James 1:17 that every good and every perfect gift comes from the Father above. God sent Jesus to show us what God is like. Jesus said, "If you've seen Me, you've seen the Father." Jeremiah 29:11 TLB says, "The plans I have for you... are plans for good and not for evil." God's wish is for our good, for us to prosper and be in health according to the level or proportion our soul prospers. It's all possible as we begin to bless the Lord.

Lindsay's Reminders:

- Pray that your words become a sweet fragrance to God and to man.

- God desires that your soul prospers.

- If you do your part, then the Lord can fulfill His.

- God has *something good* planned for you.

CHAPTER 8

Walk Through It

Some time ago I faced a physical problem that was overwhelming. I was in the center of a healing ministry, yet for more than a year and a half my prayers seemed to be hitting the ceiling and bouncing straight back.

Night after night I cried out to God for a miracle.

One day I turned on the television, and Jerry Savelle was preaching on faith. He asked, "What happens when you stand in one place and say, yes and amen—yet on the other side is where you receive the physical manifestation of what you are believing for?"

Night after night I cried out to God for a miracle.

Then Jerry asked this question: "What is the distance between *here*, the place of God's promise in prayer, and *there*, where you actually receive the answer? What is it called?"

I looked at the television set and shouted out loud, "Jerry, it's called *hell*—that's what it is! It's called the big one, the black hole, the towering inferno, the pit!"

I knew it was hell because I had been walking through it for eighteen long months.

Jerry looked into the camera, and he was speaking directly to me. He said, "No. It's called obtaining the character and nature of God."

I kept talking to the television. "You are wrong, Jerry," I said. "It's hell!" And to me it certainly was a living hell on earth.

A Different Path

Let me be clear. I believe in surgery. Doctors are wonderful and vital to our health care. And I had been to several doctors, hospitals, and emergency rooms. However, I kept feeling that the things they agreed on as being wrong were not the *only* problems.

Although the doctors did diagnose certain things consistently, I knew in my spirit that those diagnoses were only one or two pieces to the whole mess. Somehow I felt there were some hidden problems not being found. But we just couldn't get *every* piece together. I knew certain things could help, but all together they were not connecting to the big puzzle—that being my life.

However, as much as I wanted an instant fix—a quick answer—the Lord kept impressing upon me that my healing would come in a different way.

I find it amazing that when most people hear a word from the Lord, they expect instant results. If it doesn't happen, they begin to question God.

My road to recovery seemed to have dangerous curves, and it was filled with potholes.

Well-meaning people say, "If this were God, it would have already happened." Or they question the Lord's timing. "Doesn't the Bible say 'in due season'?" Yet which one of us knows God's due season unless He reveals it to us. One person's due season may not be the same for another. The final authority is God, and He knows and sees everything—the beginning from the end. But finding my due season seemed like an impossible dream.

I Was Confused

Month after month I struggled. There were times I made great progress. Then I would slide back to square one. My road to recovery seemed to have dangerous curves, and it was filled with potholes.

I was confused.

My physical body felt as though it were literally falling apart. My weight was shrinking, and the color of my skin began to turn a strange shade of gray. I would do my best to act well when, in fact, I had to struggle to get through the day.

I knew there were things I could do surgically, yet I had no peace about it. And most important to me, I had such a conviction in my heart that God was doing something differently. It's hard to explain.

In no way did God cause me to be sick. I knew sickness and disease were attacks of the devil. Yet I also knew (for some reason that is extremely difficult to put into words on paper) that God was taking me to a different place in my spiritual walk.

For me it was a very unusual experience in unconditional trust. God would say, "Do this," or "Go here," or whatever, and that would be the activity deal for the day. It was a very unusual direct, day-to-day walk with God.

It's hard to explain, but it was a wonderful experience in walking close to God in spite of the physical mess—or maybe because of it. In the midst of all this, I heard the most unusual sermon on faith. Faith is best demonstrated in the storm. For how can you ever know God to be a healer if you've never been sick? Or how can you know Him to be a way-maker unless you've been lost?

The greatest light is the one that's seen in the darkness. The highest mountain always looks higher after focusing on the lowest valley. Each step of faith was more and more precious as the days went on. Each victory was sweeter when the struggle seemed unusually hard.

The only way to prove you really know the answers to the tough questions is by taking a test. Well, I was certainly being put to the test, and I cherished each time I smelled the sweet fragrance of victory.

"You Are Wenting!"

One day God spoke to my heart and said, "I am taking you on a journey of faith."

I called my father-in-law, Oral Roberts, who was in California, and he had the most remarkable word for me.

He said, "Lindsay, you are *wenting!*"

> *If this was to be a journey of faith, then it also must be a journey of the Word.*

"Wenting?" I responded. "What in the world is that?"

He said, "Some people in the Bible were healed instantly, and I am all for that." Then he added, "But some were healed *as they went.*" (Luke 17:14.) He repeated, "You are *wenting!*"

The Lord began to tell me, "You are going to walk this one out."

The Healing Word

In order to walk this journey of faith out to the end, I had come to realize one thing—that I needed to find within me the faith that was necessary for the job at hand. Well, I knew that Romans 10:17 says, "Faith cometh by hearing, and hearing by the word of God." If this was to be a journey of faith, then it also must be a journey of the Word. So I decided to dig, jump, plunge, and immerse myself in the Word of God. I found Scriptures that were life to me, and I began to ingest them like a hungry man with bread.

And the Scriptures that I believe saved my life are those we discussed in chapter five. "My son, attend to my words; incline thine ear unto my sayings. Let them not depart from thine eyes; keep them in the midst of thine heart. For they are life unto those that find them, and health to all their flesh. Keep thy heart with all diligence; for out of it are the issues of life" (Prov. 4:20-23).

My family joined with me in agreement that God would do a miraculous work in my body.

I was given a book by Dodie Osteen titled *Healed of Cancer,* and I underlined about forty Scriptures on healing. I began to read them out loud four times a day—that's about 160 Scriptures. And that was like a spiritual appetizer. The more I read, the more I wanted to read. The more I read, the hungrier I'd get for more. I was not kidding with the Lord nor with the devil, who is the author of sickness and disease and my enemy.

"Lindsay Is Healed"

I read the words of the prophet Isaiah, who said about the coming Messiah, "He was wounded for our transgressions, he was bruised for our iniquities: the chastisement of our peace was upon him; and with his stripes we are healed" (Isa. 53:5).

I began to quote those words not four times, but 400 times every day.

I placed my own name in that verse and began to say, "By the stripes that wounded Jesus, Lindsay is healed and every bit whole."

I began to quote those words not four times, but *400 times* every day. I kept a little notebook with me at all times, and I would place a check mark in the book each time I would quote that Scripture until my 400 Scriptures were accomplished daily.

Confessing the Word

Hundreds of times every day I confessed those words over my body. I continued to read those forty Scriptures four times a day. Plus, I quoted Psalm 21:2, Psalm 23, Psalm 91, and Psalm 103:1-5 as follows:

Thou hast given him his heart's desire, and hast not withheld the request of his lips.

PSALM 21:2

The Lord is my shepherd; I shall not want. He maketh me to lie down in green pastures: he leadeth me beside the still waters. He restoreth my soul: he leadeth me in the paths of righteousness for his name's sake. Yea, though I walk through the valley of the shadow of death, I will fear no evil: for thou art with me; thy rod and thy staff they comfort me. Thou preparest a table before me in the presence of mine enemies: thou anointest my head with oil; my cup runneth over. Surely goodness and mercy shall follow me all the days of my life: and I will dwell in the house of the Lord forever.

PSALM 23:1-6

He that dwelleth in the secret place of the most High shall abide under the shadow of the Almighty. I will say of the Lord, He is my refuge and my fortress: my God; in him will I trust. Surely he shall deliver thee from the snare of the fowler, and from the noisome pestilence. He shall cover thee with his feathers, and under his wings shalt thou trust: his truth shall be thy shield and buckler.

PSALM 91:1-4

Thou shalt not be afraid for the terror by night; nor for the arrow that flieth by day; nor for the pestilence that walketh in darkness; nor for the destruction that wasteth at noonday. A thousand shall fall at thy side, and ten thousand at thy right hand; but it shall not come nigh thee. Only with thine eyes shalt thou behold and see the reward of the wicked.

PSALM 91:5-8

Because thou hast made the Lord, which is my refuge, even the most High, thy habitation; there shall no evil befall thee, neither shall any plague come nigh thy dwelling. For he shall give his angels charge over thee, to keep thee in all thy ways. They shall bear thee up in their hands, lest thou dash thy foot against a stone. Thou shalt tread upon the lion and adder: the young lion and the dragon shalt thou trample under feet.

PSALM 91:9-13

The Word revolutionized our family.

Because he hath set his love upon me, therefore will I deliver him: I will set him on high, because he hath known my name. He shall call upon me, and I will answer him: I will be with him in trouble; I will deliver him, and honour him. With long life will I satisfy him, and show him my salvation.

PSALM 91:14-16

Bless the Lord, O my soul: and all that is within me, bless his holy name. Bless the Lord, O my soul, and forget not all his benefits: who forgiveth all thine iniquities; who healeth all thy diseases; who redeemeth thy life from destruction; who crowneth thee with loving-kindness and tender mercies; who satisfieth thy mouth with good things; so that thy youth is renewed like the eagle's.

PSALM 103:1-5

A Family Adventure

The Word revolutionized our family. My mother joined in every day. She quoted each Scripture over me just as we all did—daily, faithfully, consistently, *every* single day without fail, without exception. The girls were quoting all these Scriptures, too. I now believe one of the reasons I was not healed instantly was so our daughters could become bathed in the Word and participate in my healing.

My children laid hands on me when I could hardly stand the pain some days. They would get up in the morning quoting their Scriptures and say, "Mommy, I've finished mine. Have you said yours yet?"

At night, Richard would come home exhausted, tired from wrestling with the enormous debt and problems at ORU. Yet he would arrive with flowers in his hand. Even though he was hurting, he was still giving and participating in my healing.

On days when I didn't want to crawl out of bed, Richard would declare by God's Word that I was the healed of the Lord no matter what it looked like.

He would begin to speak Scripture over me.

The Promise

Those days were memorable steps on my journey, and I had already been through plenty in my life. By my eighteenth birthday, I had already been told by a physician, "Lindsay, you will never be able to have children." By twenty-five, I was in the hospital with a cyst on my only functioning ovary. The doctor had me in surgery to remove the cyst and anything it was attached to. He had prepared Richard and me for a total hysterectomy, and things were not going as I had planned.

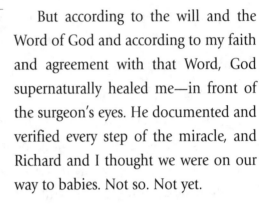

Many escape and say, "Thank God, we survived the war." They never experience the thrill of victory.

But according to the will and the Word of God and according to my faith and agreement with that Word, God supernaturally healed me—in front of the surgeon's eyes. He documented and verified every step of the miracle, and Richard and I thought we were on our way to babies. Not so. Not yet.

Next came two miscarriages and the death of our son, who lived only thirty-six hours. He was born perfectly healthy, pronounced perfectly normal, and in less than two days he was perfectly dead. There was no medical explanation whatsoever.

The Lord reminded me of how He sent Elijah and Elisha through Gilgal, and it was horrible. He sent them through Bethel, and it was even worse. Then, on to Jericho, a place of war. Finally, Elijah was about to travel alone to the Jordan River, but Elisha said, "As the Lord lives and as your soul lives, I will not leave you. And the two of them went on" (2 Kings 2:6 AMP).

Many escape and say, "Thank God, we survived the war." They never experience the thrill of victory. I told God, "I went through Gilgal, Bethel, and Jericho. Now I want my Jordan."

We finally experienced the miracle birth of our daughter, and you already know the name I gave to our first child that lived—Jordan. It means "crossing to the other side" and "obtaining the promise of God."

Totally Restored

Now, after months of facing a physical challenge, I told the Lord, "You've performed miracles for me in the past, and I am standing on Your promises again."

Morning, noon, and night I was confessing and walking, claiming and *wenting*.

Slowly, the miracle began to happen. The condition began to subside, and my health was being restored. Every day I lifted my hands to heaven and exclaimed, "Lord, I will never stop praising You for the power of Your Word!" And to this day, thanking and praising God for each day of abundant life is still a vital part of my day.

Your Supply

Perhaps you are in a dead-end situation and believe there is absolutely no way out physically, financially, emotionally, or in some area in your family. Well, don't despair. I can tell you from personal experience that I attached myself to the Scripture that declares, "My God shall supply all your need according to his riches in glory by Christ Jesus" (Phil. 4:19). When we get into obedience and expectation of God's Word, things begin to happen.

The Lord did not promise that the journey would be uneventful. You may find yourself traveling through your own Gilgal, Bethel, and Jericho.

But be encouraged. The peaceful waters of the Jordan can be on the other side.

Lindsay's Reminders:

- Jesus healed many "as they went."

- You can "walk out" your miracle.

- Confess God's Word daily.

- If we call, the Lord can answer.

- God can lead you through the storm.

- The Lord is fully able to supply *all* of your needs.

When the answer isn't instant and the outcome isn't sure, your steps are still ordered of the Lord. Through His will and His Word you can walk through it.

CHAPTER 9

"Oh, My Word!"

My grandmother was quite a character. Her name was Pauline, but we called her Grandma Charlie. Charlie was my grandfather's name, and my niece lovingly called him Grandpa Charlie. So if he was Grandpa Charlie, she was Grandma Charlie, and the name stuck. From then on, Pauline was Grandma Charlie to every one of us.

She has been in heaven many years, yet I will never forget this unforgettable woman. She was short in stature but stands tall in my memory, especially for the unique way in which she kept in touch with us.

She lived in Alabama and would often write letters to us. However, it was a challenge for our family to read her entire message. There were four of us: my mom, Patricia; my sister, Stephanie; my brother, Harry; and me. My father died when I was twelve.

Instead of sending each of us a letter, she would write just one four-page epistle and mail each of us only one page. What a hoot!

At the bottom of my page it might read, "Your Grandpa Charlie, he...", and that would be the end. I would phone my mom and say, "Did you get the page that said what Charlie did?"

"No," she would answer. "I received the part that talked about her neighbor. She must have sent that to Stephanie or Harry." So I would phone them.

The more you read Scripture, the more you know the Almighty.

With each letter, we would go through the same routine, and we'd chuckle at our grandma.

We'd call her, and she would laugh and say, "I knew you were wondering who had the next line."

Her personality was reflected not only in her words, but in her actions. Mailing four-page letters, one page per person in four different directions, always brought us laughter to share with each other. Grandma knew exactly what she was doing. It was her way of expressing her personality and *everyone* got a good laugh out of it.

There's No Mistake

That's how it is with God. His character and nature are found in the Word. And He loves to express who He is.

How do we know that the still, small voice we hear is coming from our Father? Very simply. After spending time with Him, we recognize His personality. He says, "Go here. Turn there. Call this person," and you know it is not anyone but your heavenly Father.

The more you read Scripture, the more you know the Almighty. Why? Because God talks like He writes, and He writes like He talks. As a result, you will begin to identify His voice.

He Can Perform It

It is through reading God's Word—a collection of His letters to people—and having continual fellowship with

Him that enables you to understand His ways and know Him *personally.*

At times, the Holy Spirit will give you amazing revelation, and you'll say, "Oh, my word!"

In reality, however, it's not your word, but His. As the truth of Scripture becomes buried in your heart, you will actually be exclaiming, "Oh, His Word!"

According to Proverbs 18:21, "Death and life are in the power of the tongue: and they that love it shall eat the fruit thereof." The Lord has given us power to speak life and death, but we are required to line up our words with His declarations, and then He can bring it to pass. As the prophet Jeremiah wrote, "Then said the Lord unto me, Thou hast well seen: for I will hasten my word to perform it" (Jer. 1:12).

The Word Made Flesh

Knowing God is a combination of hearing, reading, and doing His Word—and receiving Christ, who is the Word made flesh.

Faith cannot live and operate in wishy-washiness.

The Creator provided more than the tangible, touchable, readable Scriptures. He sent His Son Jesus, the Word clothed in the form of man. "The Word was made flesh, and dwelt among us, (and we beheld his glory, the glory as of the only begotten of the Father,) full of grace and truth" (John 1:14).

Mixed Signals

Some people give the Lord mixed signals. They declare, "I can do all things through Christ who strengthens me." Then Satan does something to trip them up, and they say, "Oh, I knew that would never work."

Their second statement then has the right to cancel out everything they have declared. As a result, their faith can waver or even be destroyed. It's the double-minded, wishy-washy state James 1:8 talks about: "A double-minded man is unstable in all his ways." And faith cannot live and operate in wishy-washiness. "Faith comes by hearing, and hearing by the word of God" (Rom. 10:17 NKJV), and God's Word isn't double minded or wishy-washy.

Remember, the words of your mouth must be *acceptable* in God's sight. They must line up with His Word.

Over His Head

If you desire to overcome stress, make it your objective to first be overcome, engulfed, completely surrounded, and immersed in the power of God.

In the book of Ezekiel there is a practical demonstration of how to become fully immersed in the things of God.

The prophet describes a vision in which he was brought to the door of a house: "Behold, waters issued out from under the threshold of the house eastward: for the forefront of the house stood toward the east, and the waters came down from under from the right side of the house, at the south side of the altar" (Ez. 47:1).

Then the water began to rise.

When he first measured, "the waters were to the ankles" (v. 3).

Soon, "the waters were to the knees" (v. 4).

Then, "the waters were to the loins" (v. 4).

Finally, it was over his head. "The waters were risen, waters to swim in, a river that could not be passed over" (v. 5).

That's how the Word should cover our life—totally. So completely that we are swimming in it.

Here's the Danger

Some people only want to wade into spiritual waters ankle deep. They are satisfied with just a little sprinkle—a little blessing here, a little anointing there. Just enough so they don't lose control.

Here lies the danger. If you walk in water only to your ankles, Satan can target almost all of your body.

Knee-deep is better, yet you can still turn around and run.

I lived in Florida long enough to learn that when you're in water up to your shoulders, you had better know how to swim.

But spiritually speaking, God wants us to take the plunge.

Many are trying to serve God with their heart, soul, mind, and strength, but they are still insisting on keeping their head above spiritual waters so their head can still be in control and make all the right *logical, carnal,* and *fleshly* decisions.

But *spiritually speaking,* God wants us to take the plunge. Get all the way under the power and authority of God in every area of our lives. I believe God wants us to totally submerge ourselves in His ways. At that stage Satan's point of attack becomes buffeted by God's anointing.

I like the phrase, "Get under the spout where the glory comes out." That's how you become totally anointed, totally blessed, totally rewarded, and totally immersed in the things of God.

Deep Waters

God encourages His people to venture beyond the shore-line and move into the deep.

When Peter, James, and John were fishing on the Sea of Galilee and had caught nothing, Jesus appeared and said to Peter, "Launch out into the deep and let down your nets for a catch" (Luke 5:4 NKJV).

And although it was not the usual, traditional way they had always done things, when the Lord spoke what was the result? They caught so many fish their nets began to break! "And they beckoned unto their partners, which were in the other ship, that they should come and help them. And they came, and filled both the ships, so that they began to sink" (Luke 5:7).

Deep spiritual waters can bring great miracles.

Satan knows he has only a little time left, and now he is really pouring on the pressure.

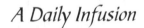

A Daily Infusion

A friend once remarked, "I love Christmas. I wish it could be every day of the year."

That's exactly how I feel about being in the presence of the Lord and immersing myself in God's Word. The traditional church service of one hour on Sunday just doesn't seem to be enough. We need a daily infusion from above. We face problems every day—sometimes throughout the entire day.

I'd like the presence and anointing of God to be with me all day so that I could make godly decisions in the face of devilish attacks.

Satan knows his time is short. The signs are everywhere that Jesus is about to return, and it's as though the devil is getting nervous. It's as if Satan knows he has only a little time left, and now he is really pouring on the pressure.

So how does Satan pour on the pressure?

He attacks finances.

He sows discord and strife.

He lies about friends and family.

He fosters jealousy and hatred.

He torments minds with fear.

Satan understands enough about the personality, character, and nature of God that he will do anything to stop you. That's why, when you are about to open your Bible, he will whisper, "You're too tired," or, "Why don't you wait till later," or, "Do you *really* understand that stuff?"

Well, about the time those feelings hit, we need to defend ourselves against the onslaught of the devil and construct a wall of protection built on a foundation of the Word.

Spiritual Warfare

Thank God, He has given us the weapons to win the battle.

For the weapons of our warfare are not carnal, but mighty through God to the pulling down of strong holds; casting down imaginations, and every high thing that exalteth itself against the knowledge of God, and bringing into captivity every thought to the obedience of Christ.

2 CORINTHIANS 10:4,5

It's not possible to defeat the strongholds of the devil by fighting in the flesh. Oh, it would be something to fight Satan with a sword—or even a baseball bat. But this is a spiritual conflict that must be fought with spiritual weapons.

We wrestle not against flesh and blood, but against principalities, against powers, against the rulers of the darkness of this world, against spiritual wickedness in high places.

EPHESIANS 6:12

The Invisible Foe

Since Satan doesn't fight fair, we must fight smart—with faith and with the knowledge of God.

What can exalt itself against the Word?

- Is it sin?

- Is it sickness?

- Is it stress?

- Is it disease?

- Is it poverty?

- Is it a court case?

Absolutely nothing should have the power to defy what God says.

No, according to the Word of God, the answer should be—*nothing.* Absolutely nothing should have the power to defy what God says. By confessing, declaring, and believing the Word, we can come against Satan's attack.

But we make the Word of God ineffective if we start doubting, worrying, fearing, or confessing the problem instead of the solution. We must know the battle is with Satan, not with people. I repeat, "We wrestle not against flesh and blood, but against principalities, against powers, against the rulers of the darkness of this world, against spiritual wickedness in high places" (Eph. 6:12).

Our fight is with the devil. To win we must exercise the weapons of our warfare. It's not a flesh fight; it's a faith fight. And the battle is the Lord's when we use our spiritual artillery according to the Word.

It is war. And we are going to be victorious.

Lindsay's Reminders:

- God's nature and character are revealed in the Scriptures.

- Jesus is the Word made flesh.

- Become engulfed in the things of God.

- Launch out into the deep.

- The Lord has given us the weapons for the battle.

- Fight with faith and the knowledge of God.

- We were created to be champions.

Today, consider stepping out of your comfort zone and becoming totally immersed in the Word of God.

CHAPTER 10

"Get A Life!"

One night several years ago while we were in Los Angeles, Richard took me to one of my favorite restaurants. We arrived in a rental car, and as we were about to walk in the door, a long white Lincoln limousine pulled to the curb.

The group that emerged received plenty of attention. They were so intoxicated they were stumbling all over each other, trying to exit the car by way of the sunroof. When they finally made it out of the car, the doorman had to help them into the restaurant.

When God told us that we could get a life, it wasn't at all in sarcasm.

Suddenly, the same doorman looked at Richard, and in a nasty voice he exclaimed, "That's that television evangelist."

I had to hold myself back to keep from making a comment of my own. I felt like repeating the same sarcastic, "Oh, get a life!" comment that we've all heard so many times when things didn't come out as desired.

But when God told us that we could get a life, it wasn't at all in sarcasm. In fact, according to the book of John, it was indeed quite the opposite.

What a Difference

God sent His Son for one reason—that you and I might have life.

Jesus said, "The thief cometh not, but for to steal, and to kill, and to destroy: I am come that they might have life, and that they might have it more abundantly" (John 10:10).

What a contrast. Satan comes to steal—which is derived from the Greek word *klepto,* as in "kleptomaniac." It fits the picture, doesn't it?

His purpose is to *kill*—to cause death, or to slaughter for any purpose.

The devil also comes to *destroy.*

He is the ultimate thief, lurking to snatch you into an eternal misery of loss, ruin, and hell. That's what he does for a living.

The devil's purpose is to steal your soul, kill your spirit, and destroy your will.

Why Would Jesus Come?

Then the Son of Man arrived with a mission exactly the opposite of the devil.

Now think about this. Why would God commission His Son, Jesus, to leave walls made out of jasper, streets made out of gold, and gates made out of pearl? Why would Jesus come to the earth and carry His cross to Golgotha, the place of the skull, where He was beaten and nails were driven into His hands? Why would the Father ask His Son to exchange the wonders of heaven to be beaten and mocked? And why

The exchange doesn't seem equal. Jesus receives my mess, and I am presented with His health, healing, peace, joy, and salvation.

would Jesus travel down the Via Dolorosa, "the way of suffering," and eventually be crucified on a cruel cross?

In this one verse Jesus gives us the answer. He declared, "I am come that they might have life, and that they might have it more abundantly."

What "life" was He talking about? Was Jesus sent that you might have breath in your body? No. Before Jesus arrived on earth, there were millions of people who had biological existence—they were alive, they were breathing.

The life Jesus referred to was *zoe* life. That is a Greek word for "life to the full"—genuine, active, vigorous, and devoted to God.

Jesus not only gives us life, but He also gives life "more abundantly"—superabundant in quantity, beyond measure, and superior in quality.

On the surface the exchange doesn't seem equal. Jesus receives my mess, and I am presented with His health, healing, peace, joy, and salvation. What an unusual, remarkably *miraculous* exchange.

Why would Jesus do that? I'm not sure as human beings we could ever fully understand that kind of unconditional, ultimate love. I can't fully comprehend it. But, praise God, because Jesus did we have an opportunity to obtain a life abundantly full of miracles while on earth and eternal, everlasting life in heaven.

It's All Ours

Abundant life includes such an overflow of wealth that it's hard to encompass it all. In fact, wealth is not just what we typically think of when we hear that word. Our society teaches us that wealth really means only a large amount of money. Yet wealth, in the fullness of its true meaning, is abundance to overflowing in all areas of your life.

The Lord has given us the riches of the earth. We are not created to be paupers when God put all the gold and silver in the earth and commanded us to subdue the earth and take dominion or control over it. That means God intended for us to have the substances He put in the earth for us. In fact, He said that when we serve and obey Him, "Then shall the earth yield her increase" (Ps. 67:6). He went on to say in Deuteronomy 8:18, "But thou shalt remember the Lord thy God: for it is he that giveth thee power to get wealth."

Third John 2 declares, "Beloved, I wish above all things that thou mayest prosper and be in health, even as thy soul prospereth." Job 36:11 says, "If

Far too many have swallowed a "poor and humble" gospel.

they obey and serve him, they shall spend their days in prosperity, and their years in pleasures."

Far too many have swallowed a "poor and humble" gospel. The emphasis, however, seems to focus on being poor, as if one supernaturally yields the other—as if poverty is worn like a crown. Yet that's not found in the Word. Many have tried to use poverty Scriptures to the advantage of twisting them and causing them to read like a great thing. Some have said the poorer you are, the more God can use you. When, actually, the poorer you are, the more poor you are. God uses the willing and obedient and even rewards those who diligently seek Him. (Heb. 11:6.)

Sowing, however, is a way of life. It's God's system that creates a lifestyle of giving and receiving according to Bible principles.

Your humility before God should remain constant regardless of the size of your bank account. However, your "flesh man" changes quickly when you can't afford lunch.

We were not born to live in poverty. The psalmist wrote, "For every beast of the forest is mine, and the cattle upon a thousand hills" (Ps. 50:10).

God desires to make you the leader, not the follower; the lender, not the borrower.

Let's face the facts. You can't lend if you don't have any money, or any lumber, or any flour.

As one man commented, "How can I lend my truck if I ain't got one?"

A Way of Life

When most believers talk about sowing and reaping, their mind immediately turns to finances. They think, *It's what I put into the offering plate that will return great dividends.* That's not worship. That's not tithing. That's "let's make a deal with God," and God isn't into spiritual deal making.

Sowing, however, is a way of life. It's God's system that creates a lifestyle of giving and receiving according to Bible principles. It's God's system of blessing, never to be confused with man's system of taking.

I recently watched a video of Oral Roberts in 1970, when he wrote the book *Miracle of Seed-Faith.* He talked about the difference between seed-faith *giving* and seed-faith *living.*

This system is not just offering God a token—or a tip—and expecting the windows of heaven to open in your direction. Seed-faith living is a lifestyle. It involves everything you have—your business, your car, your job, your finances, your prayers, your influence, even your smile. It's living to give because it's godly.

"*I Loved That Car*"

I've had a firsthand understanding of the miracle of seed-faith because I've lived it for years. Recently, however, I experienced it in an awesome dimension.

For about two years I had needed another car. Mine was eight years old and had over 65,000 miles on it.

I loved that car, and I really hated the thought of selling it. For so long nothing went wrong, and I was concerned about changing cars when I had such a dependable one. But now enough things were going wrong that I knew we would soon be facing repair bills.

In my spirit I felt I should change cars, but I felt a check about selling it.

I told Richard, "We need to pray about the car." And we did.

He said, "Lindsay, you've got to get another car."

"Well, I know that," I told him, "but I don't know if I'm supposed to fix it and sell it, or give the car away." So, when in doubt, I wait on God.

Was This the Lord?

What the Lord told me next hit me like a thunderbolt. He placed the name of a person before me and said, "Call her and tell her you are going to begin to pay her car payment."

"Lord, You've got to be kidding. She drives a BMW," I responded. Then I began to think, *Hmm, maybe it's paid for.* NOT! But I really knew this was God. I *really* knew I was supposed to do this.

So I made the call, and during the conversation I hesitantly asked, "By the way, do you own your car?"

"No," she said, "I pay car payments."

I said, "Well, the Lord spoke to me and told me to start paying those for you."

When I found out the amount, I said, "Lord, what are You getting me into?" But I *knew* it was God. Now keep this in mind. My car was in need of repair or sale, it was eight years old and had 65,000 miles on it, and I'm to pay payments on someone else's car. Go figure God!

Within a few months I had sowed enough to have financed a trade for myself, yet that's *not* what the Lord instructed.

But my own car problems didn't stop. In fact, they began to really multiply until one day the car just died.

"That's It!"

So, as always, I called Richard. He got right to work on finding the problem and where to have it fixed. In the meantime, I got rides and borrowed cars—mostly Richard's car.

After my car was repaired, it happened again. This time it was a hit-and-run in a parking lot. It's a good thing they ran. Oh, I was so disheartened. I mean, I thought, *Lord, I'm hot, I'm tired, I'm car-towed, I'm paying someone else's car payment, and now this!* But, as usual, I prayed and called Richard. Again, we fixed it, but then it started overheating.

Then one hot 105-degree summer day, the car overheated again. I called Richard and said, "My car either has to be towed or someone needs to figure out what to do with it."

Just when Richard was ready to make the deal, suddenly the Spirit of God rose up in me and cautioned, "Not yet!"

"Lindsay, that's it!" said an exasperated Richard. "I'm taking you to the car dealership."

In my spirit I still wasn't completely sure what to do, but it appeared in the natural that it was time to trade. So we drove to the car lot.

Richard and I began to look around and ask questions, and finally he said, "What's your dream car?"

I walked right over to it, looked at the sticker price, and said, "Hello!"

Then Richard said, "Okay now, let's be realistic." So we went to the used car lot and found one that was like my dream car—only it was four or five years old. It had reasonable mileage, and with my car as a trade in, it was easily a price we could afford.

So I agreed, "Okay, we can trade in my car, and I can afford this—especially if I don't have to pay someone else's payments." Ha! Well, not so fast.

Just when Richard was ready to make the deal, suddenly the Spirit of God rose up in me and cautioned, "Not yet!"

I turned to my husband and whispered, "Let's go home. God said, 'Not yet!'"

The look on his face communicated, "Okay, I know God said that to you, but, honey, right now you're either walking or getting a ride. We have got to think this through."

I knew Richard was tired of me borrowing his car, and I told him, "We're going to pray until we get a clear direction from the Lord."

"Not Yet"

Meanwhile, my car was grounded, and I was making payments on another woman's BMW. Still, God kept repeating those two words, "Not yet!"

One night, after again having my car repaired, I was on my way to our live eight o'clock television program, when my car stalled out once more.

When I finally arrived, for some reason, instead of being frustrated, I began to chuckle.

"Where have you been?" asked Richard.

"My car is broken. It did it again." I couldn't stop laughing. He thought I had flipped.

"I Really Don't Know"

A man in the studio overheard me. He was from out of state and had been in the building where my car was. "What's the matter with your car?" he asked.

"I really don't know," I answered between my laughs.

He began to ask me one question after another, and the more he asked, the more I felt a release from God not to care, not to worry. When God said we were to cast our cares upon

Him, I really did. It wasn't that I didn't care, I just didn't care! A car was not going to make me forget God's Word, forget His voice, or forget His promises.

Well, this man continued the conversation, asking me all kinds of car questions about all possible car situations. My best answer was your basic, "I don't know."

"What kind of car do you want?"

"I really don't know," I replied still chuckling.

"Well, tell me about your dream car."

So I told him.

"What's your favorite car color?" he asked.

"White."

"What color interior?"

"Tan." Having no idea this man had a person behind him writing all these details down, I went ahead and appeared on the program that evening.

"Turn In Here"

Over the days ahead I continued to feel led of God to give away several other major things I owned. I did it in obedience as God directed, and I considered each one as a seed to Him.

God isn't looking for our greatness. He's a great God who is looking for our obedience.

About two weeks later my brother—under the guise of buying his wife a car—took me to a car dealership with him. When we arrived, there stood not only the man I had talked to earlier, but my husband and children...and my dream car! He was giving me a brand-new car! When I became obedient to God, I began to share in His abundance.

The "O" Word

What does the Lord honor? It's the "O" word—obedience. So many times we think we've got the plan, or we've got to figure out a plan, or do something we're just not capable of doing in our human flesh. But God isn't looking for our greatness. He's a great God who is looking for our obedience.

One thing I've learned over years and years of experiences—some good, some not so good—is that God honors obedience. He gave us His system. When we obey the system,

God is more than faithful to do His part. In fact, He is a rewarder of those who diligently seek Him. God enjoys blessing and rewarding those who seek Him. In fact, as far as the solution to stress is concerned, God rewarding His people becomes quite simple when we seek Him.

Physically and spiritually Jesus came so that we could trade what we are for everything He is.

In John 14:27, Jesus declares, "Peace I leave with you, my peace I give unto you: not as the world giveth, give I unto you. Let not your heart be troubled, neither let it be afraid." And the word *peace* here means "a harmonious relationship between God and man."

When we diligently seek God, He rewards us with the kind of peace that can come only from the Prince of Peace Himself. Then it's a peace that does not come from the world, and therefore, it cannot be taken away by the world. God's peace brings oneness and wholeness.

The Exchange

People have told me, "I can't wait to get rid of this pressure, and I think I know how to do it."

Weeks or months later, the stress is still there. Do you know why? Because if *you* try to empty yourself of a problem, there will be a vacuum—and the same pressure will rush back in to fill the void.

Instead, consider exchanging that trouble for something completely different.

Jesus laid down His life as a substitute for everything that we are—our imperfections, our temper, our gloom-and-doom, our attitude, our anxiety—everything. Physically and spiritually Jesus came so that we could trade what we are for everything He is.

Jesus is all-sufficient, "able to do exceeding abundantly above all that we ask or think" (Eph. 3:20).

When you release yourself to Jesus you:

- Exchange your sorrow for His salvation.

- Exchange your problems for His provision.

- Exchange your burdens for His blessings.

- Exchange your stress for His strength.

Think of it. The highest and best—which Christ is—was freely imparted. He gives to those in Christ everything that He is in exchange for everything that they are.

It's Not Yours

Today, if you are still carrying poverty, sickness, discouragement, disease, devastation, and stress, it's *not* yours. And it's certainly not yours anymore if you choose to receive all that Jesus went to the cross for. You are holding on to the wrong package. He freely exchanged it two thousand years ago.

If you picked up the wrong package at a department store, surely you wouldn't hesitate to go back and exchange it. I would exchange anything that didn't belong to me.

But can you imagine how quickly we'd exchange something that was just a raw deal? I mean, if you paid for a diamond and they sent you dust, that would be a raw deal. And you'd be quick to make the correct exchange. Well, Satan has tried to make us accept a raw deal, and I want to encourage you to make a proper exchange for anything and everything Jesus already paid for in your behalf more than two thousand years ago.

Basically, Satan is running off with your blessing. Most likely God is not happy about it, and neither should you be. If Jesus went to the cross in your behalf, then all He paid for that's rightfully yours should now in fact be yours.

That means that what God sent Jesus to purchase with His shed blood—healing, health, prosperity, peace of mind, soundness, oneness, wholeness, everything He paid for—is waiting, just waiting for the right exchange to be made. But it's up to us. God has done His part; now it's up to us to receive all He has already paid the price for.

> *If you are still plagued by sin, sorrow, and stress, isn't it time to "get a life"?*

What Jesus brought us was from heaven, where there is no sorrow, no sadness, no pain. So the question becomes this: Why are you living your old life when Jesus gave you a new one?

Jesus Christ came to take what there was in Lindsay Roberts' life before she accepted Jesus and replace it with everything He had in heaven. He brought it *with* Him and freely made the trade at Calvary. He took the stripes on His back and declared, "It is finished!" And it was.

He said, "Lindsay, I not only want to give you life, but also life more abundantly." It is beyond measure, super-abundant in quantity, and superior in quality.

Your New Life

If you are still plagued by sin, sorrow, and stress, isn't it time to "get a life"? To freely exchange all that's going on in your life for the life that was given to you when Jesus went to Calvary?

Lindsay's Reminders

- It is Satan who comes to steal, kill, and destroy.

- Jesus came to give us life.

- Abundance in every area of life is included in the Lord's plan.

- Seed-faith living should become our lifestyle.

- Jesus brought the best of heaven as a gift for you and me.

- God's provision is available so we can exchange our human stress for His godly strength.

I am praying that any anxiety, stress, worry, or fear in your life will be exchanged for the peace of God that our Savior has already provided—that His sweet peace which passes our human understanding will become your portion today. (Phil. 4:7.)

I believe God's provision in His Word declares that on the authority of God's Word it really is possible to experience abundant life. Now it's up to us to seek out His will and do it.

Psalm 31:19 says, "Oh how great is thy goodness, which thou hast laid up for them that fear thee; which thou hast wrought for them that trust in thee before the sons of men!"

How great is God's goodness. As my father-in-law always says, "God is a good God!" But this verse goes on to say He is not only a good God, but how *great* is His goodness. And that great goodness is laid up for us when we fear Him. Now the word *fear* in this instance doesn't mean you're afraid of God. Don't miss what this verse says because our words are translated a little differently. Fear simply means to revere or have reverence for God.

As we reverence and trust and look to God, He pours out His goodness. It goes on in verse 24 to say, "Be of good courage, and he shall strengthen your heart, all ye that hope in the Lord." When our hope is in the Lord, He strengthens us. God strengthens our heart.

Romans 10:10 says, "With the heart man believeth unto righteousness; and with the mouth confession is made unto salvation." So by strengthening our heart, our ability to believe is strengthened also. We can believe right and believe stronger as God strengthens our heart.

We are not to be faint-hearted. (Deut. 20:3,4.) But we're to be strong *in the Lord* (thank God, it's in the Lord

140

and not in our own strength) and in the power of His might. (Eph. 6:10.)

There's power in the Lord—mighty power. When we apply God's strength and mighty power to any situation we face, He has the power to change our circumstances. When we attach ourselves to God and to His mighty power, that's when miracles begin to happen. With God and His mighty power and His great goodness, we can overcome Satan's attacks and defeat the devil, even in the area of stress. With God's help, I believe we truly can be *blessed* and not stressed.

When we attach ourselves to God and to His mighty power, that's when miracles begin to happen.

Let's pray.

Heavenly Father, I pray for the precious one reading this book and this prayer. I come to You, joining them in believing for a miracle in the area of stress, and I am asking for Your divine intervention. I thank You for it in Jesus' mighty name. Amen.

Now I want you to pray this as a declaration before God, and let Satan hear it as well.

I declare that the Word of God is true, that Jesus went to the cross and died for my sins and my shortcomings. I believe that as the Son of God, who rose from the dead, Jesus has the power and authority to heal me, to deliver me, and to set me free in every area of my life—and that includes stress. I use my faith to come against stress, and I have a Bible right to command Satan to let me go free of stress.

So, Satan, take your hands off me in every area. I'm God's property, not yours. And as His child, I exercise my Bible right to healing and declare as a statement of my faith that I have a right to overcome stress. I make a declaration of my faith that I, too, can be blessed, not stressed, according to God's Word, in Jesus' name. Amen and amen.

I am truly praying for God to use the words in this book, the prayer you just prayed, His Holy Word, and your faith to be a winning combination to overcome stress in your life.

It's my prayer for God to richly bless you spiritually, physically, financially, emotionally, and in every area of your life. I pray that from this day on you will live a life that is truly blessed, not stressed.

Prayer of Salvation

God loves you—no matter who you are, no matter what your past. God loves you so much that He gave His One and only begotten Son for you. The Bible tells us that "...whoever believes in him shall not perish but have everlasting life" (John 3:16 NIV). Jesus laid down His life and rose again so that we could spend eternity with Him in heaven and experience His absolute best on earth. If you would like to receive Jesus into your life, say the following prayer out loud and mean it from your heart.

Heavenly Father, I come to You admitting that I am a sinner. Right now, I choose to turn away from sin, and I ask You to cleanse me of all unrighteousness. I believe that Your Son, Jesus, died on the cross to take away my sins. I also believe that He rose again from the dead so that I might be forgiven of my sins and made righteous through faith in Him. I call upon the name of Jesus Christ to be the Savior and Lord of my life. Jesus, I choose to follow You and ask that You fill me with the power of the Holy Spirit. I declare that right now I am a child of God. I am free from sin and full of the righteousness of God. I am saved in Jesus' name. Amen.

If you prayed this prayer to receive Jesus Christ as your Savior for the first time, please contact us on the web at **www.harrisonhouse.com** to receive a free book.

Or you may write to us at:
Harrison House
P.O. Box 35035
Tulsa, Oklahoma 74153

About the Author

After her marriage to Richard in 1980, Lindsay began traveling with her husband, ministering throughout the world, and supporting him in what the Lord has called him to do.

"After the birth of our son, Richard Oral," Lindsay says, "we were devastated when he lived only 36 hours. But God picked us up, dried our tears, and helped us try again." Out of that experience from pain to victory, Lindsay wrote *36 Hours With an Angel*—the story of how God sustained their faith after Richard Oral's death and blessed her and Richard with the miracle birth of their three daughters: Jordan, Olivia, and Chloe.

Lindsay hosts "Make Your Day Count," a daily television program full of ministry, cooking, creative tips, and lots of fun. With her husband, Richard, she also co-hosts the nightly television program, "The Hour of Healing."

She has co-authored several books, such as *A Cry for Miracles* and *Dear God, I Love To Eat, But I Sure Do Hate To Cook* cookbook. She has also written several children's books, including *ABC's of Faith for Children* and *God's Champions*.

Lindsay serves as editor of *Make Your Day Count*, a quarterly magazine aimed at today's woman; *Miracles Now*, a quarterly magazine for ministry partners; and *Your Daily Guide to Miracles*, a daily devotional book published semi-annually.

She is a member of the Oral Roberts University Board of Regents.

"I am dedicated to God and willing to do whatever He calls me to do," Lindsay says. "I also stand in support of the call of God upon my husband. He and I are both grateful that God is using us for His glory."

To contact Lindsay Roberts
please write to:

Lindsay Roberts
c/o Oral Roberts Ministries
Tulsa, OK 74171-0001
or
e-mail her at:
Lindsay@orm.cc

Please include your prayer requests
and comments when you write.

If you would like to have someone join in agreement with you in prayer as a point of contact, consider calling the Abundant Life Prayer Group at **918-495-7777**. They are there to pray with you twenty-four hours a day, seven days a week.

Additional copies of this book
are available from your local bookstore.

If this book has been a blessing to you,
or if you would like to see more of
the Harrison House product line,
please visit us on our website at
www.harrisonhouse.com.

HARRISON HOUSE
Tulsa, Oklahoma 74153

The Harrison House Vision

Proclaiming the truth and the power

Of the Gospel of Jesus Christ

With excellence;

Challenging Christians to

Live victoriously,

Grow spiritually,

Know God intimately.